ONE HUNDRED YEARS OF WOMEN'S GOLF

The Ladies' Golf Union's headquarters in St Andrews. The LGU came to St Andrews after their spell in Sandwich Bay in Kent. Orginally in rented premises overlooking the eighteenth green of the Old Course, they then purchased this impressive property on The Scores. The house is but a pitch shot away from the R&A, whose assistance down the years has been much appreciated

ONE HUNDRED YEARS OF WOMEN'S GOLF

LEWINE MAIR

Foreword by

HRH The Duke of York

MAINSTREAM
PUBLISHING

EDINBURGH AND LONDON

in conjunction with

First published in Great Britain 1992 by
MAINSTREAM PUBLISHING COMPANY (EDINBURGH) LTD
7 Albany Street
Edinburgh EH1 3UG

ISBN 1 85158 427 7 (cloth)

A catalogue record for this book is available from the British Library

Typeset in Monotype Bembo 11/14pt by CentraCet, Cambridge

Printed in Great Britain by Butler & Tanner Ltd, Frome

Contents

Acknowledgements

The author and the LGU would like to thank the following for their co-operation: Bridget Jackson; Lady Heathcoat-Amory; JoAnne Carner; Laura Davies; Liz Pook; Guy Robertson-Durham; Stewart Lawson; David Pearson; Zara Bolton; Pat Turvey; Philomena Garvey; *The Scotsman*; *Golf Monthly*; Enid Wilson; Mary McKenna; Belle Robertson; Barry Edwards; Louise Suggs; Elaine Farquharson; Colin Farquharson; Barbara McIntosh; Ruth Ferguson; Wendy Russell; Norman Mair; Sally Hepburn; Alma Robertson and Joan Neville.

Lady Margaret Scott and the championship cup she won from 1893–1895

Bibliography

Barton, Pamela, *A Stroke a Hole*, Blackies, 1937

Boys, Miss M., *Our Lady of the Green*, 1899

Collett, Glenna, *Ladies in the Rough*, 1929

Cossey, Rosalynde, *Golfing Ladies*, Orbis 1984

Crane, M., *The Story of Ladies' Golf*, Stanley Paul, 1991

Darwin, Bernard, *Golf Between Two Wars*, Chatto and Windus, 1944

Helme, Eleanor, *After the Ball*, Hurst and Blackett, 1931

Hezlet, May, *Ladies' Golf*, Hutchinson, 1904

Houghton, George, *Golf Addict Among the Scots*, Country Life, 1967

Hutchinson, Horace G., *Golf*, Badminton Library, 1890

Moran, Frank, *Golfers' Gallery*, Oliver and Boyd, 1946

Steel, Donald, *The Bedside Book of Golf*, Batsford Books, 1971

Steel, D. and Ryde, P., *The Shell International Encyclopedia of Golf*, Ebury Press, 1975

Stringer, Mabel, *Golfing Reminiscences*, Mills and Boon, 1924

Taylor, J. H., *Taylor on Golf*, Hutchinson, 1902

Valentine, Jessie, *Better Golf Definitely*, Pelham, 1967

Wethered, Miss J., *Golfing Memories and Methods*, Hutchinson, 1933

Wilson, Enid, *A Gallery of Women Golfers*, Country Life, 1961

Zaharias, Babe Didrickson, *This Life I've Led*, Robert Hale, 1956

Foreword

by HRH The Duke of York

Golf is a game which has spanned both the years and the generations. Although a great deal has changed in a century, not least in the development of equipment, I think it is safe to say that our forebears suffered as much frustration over a swirling six-foot putt as do golfers of today. I dare say that a similar view will be taken a hundred years from now. Golf has a timeless quality and it gives me great pleasure to write a foreword to this book which marks a century of women's golf.

Golf has much to recommend it both to the players and followers of the game alike. It provides a test of patience, application, perseverance and character for players at all levels and is played in virtually every corner of the world. It is a fully international game which is on offer to anyone, from whatever walk of life, who is physically able to try his or her skill at the game.

The international scope of the game has benefited me enormously and I have been lucky enough to play in many parts of the world, in places as far apart as Iceland and Hong Kong. It is a social game but it also has the ability to afford solitude when you only require to play a few holes on your own in order to refresh the mind and to escape the madding crowd.

One of the many advantages of golf is that it is essentially a game of skill and timing and players need not depend on any special physique to succeed. It is a game of equal opportunities and, with discrimination against women becoming a thing of the past, I hope golf will blossom and flourish to an even greater extent in the next one hundred years.

Issette Pearson on the first tee at St Anne's On Sea during the first British Ladies' Championship, 1893

Introduction

The Ladies' Golf Union is indebted to Lewine Mair, the *Daily Telegraph*'s women's golf correspondent, for writing our Centenary book. She has pieced together key moments and key players in a manner which captures the excitement of the women's game and the spirit in which it has been played for the last hundred years.

In addition to thanking the writer, I would personally like to pay tribute to the countless voluntary workers – from Issette Pearson, the first Secretary, to those good ladies in office today at club, county and national level – who have kept the LGU on course. Their time and expertise have been crucial to our development as, indeed, has the assistance we have received from our neighbours in St Andrews, the R&A.

To the women who run the handicap system within the clubs, I should like to give a special vote of thanks. It is difficult enough to keep tabs on one's own handicap, let alone an entire membership's. Yet those at the helm cope splendidly with what is, at times, a particularly heavy workload.

The junior co-ordinator is another whose role in the scheme of things is maybe not fully appreciated.

Apart from my present position as President, I have been privileged to captain many teams, including the Curtis Cup sides of 1978 and 1980. Having seen so much, for so long, I am in a position to be well aware of improved standards among the young.

For this upward spiral to have occurred, much has to be right with the framework. Today we have a situation where a club official will direct girls into the junior county arena, and at county level there are those who can put juniors in the picture where the national and British Under–18 championships are concerned.

The top youngster of the 1990s will have as much fun as her forbears. The Curtis Cup is one match at which she can aim; the Vagliano Trophy and Commonwealth Tournaments two more. They are events which, among them, could take a player round the world.

But, globally or locally, there is something in this great game for everyone.

And, when a golfer's day is done, scratch and handicap players alike will still be talking the same language; dwelling on friendships made across the years.

Carol Comboy
President Ladies' Golf Union

CHAPTER ONE

In The Beginning

North Berwick
9th April 1893

Dear Miss Martin,

I have read your letter about the proposed Ladies' Golf Union with much interest. Let me give you the famous advice of Mr Punch (since you honour me by asking for my opinion). DON'T. My reasons? Well!

1) Women never have and never can unite to push any scheme to success. They are bound to fall out and quarrel on the smallest or no provocation; they are built that way!

2) They will never go through one Ladies' Championship with credit. Tears will bedew, if wigs do not bestrew, the green.

3) Constitutionally and physically women are unfitted for golf. They will never last through two rounds of a long course in a day. Nor can they ever hope to defy the wind and weather encountered on our best links even in spring and summer. Temperamentally the strain will be too great for them. THE FIRST LADIES' CHAMPIONSHIP WILL BE THE LAST, unless I and others are greatly mistaken. The L.G.U. seems scarcely worthwhile. . . .

Thus wrote Horace Hutchinson, a leading British amateur of the day, to Blanche Martin, the lady destined to be the LGU's first treasurer. In so doing, he provided the golfing pioneers with precisely the kind of impetus they needed to get their scheme underway.

Not only was the LGU founded within a matter of weeks, but the first British Women's championship began on 13 June of that same year at the Ladies' Course of the St Anne's Golf Club.

Such were the first steps to formalise the distaff side of a game which, three centuries before, had captured the imagination of Mary Queen of Scots. Her Royal Highness was a keen exponent, albeit one whose career was dramatically cut short when she failed to maintain that relationship between head and shoulders which all the game's great teachers have deemed essential.

Not all the early golfers belonged to the aristocracy – the fishwives of Musselburgh, for example, ran a thriving golf club in the late 1700s.

These women, who also indulged in football, would compete for such commodities as fishing baskets and Barcelona silk handkerchiefs. Such prizes would seem to be along not dissimilar lines to those handed out at today's open meetings and, just as, in recent times, the former British champion and Curtis Cup captain, Jill Thornhill, built up a store of eight coffee sets, so one can imagine the winning fisherwoman murmuring, 'not another handkerchief'. Although the fisherwomen doubtless had the wrists to give the ball a healthy whack, one suspects that any attempt at hard hitting did little for their reputations.

Up at St Andrews, at the time when the first Ladies' Club was being started, a golfing female was viewed as a woman of ill-repute. 'A damsel with even one modest putter in her hand,' recorded Miss A. M. Steward in *The Gentlewoman's Book of Sports*, 'was labelled a fast and almost disreputable person, definitely one to be avoided.'

It is as well that Laura Davies, who not so long ago hit a drive and five iron aboard a par five of 575 yards in the Hawaiian Open, was not around when Lord Moncrieff solemnly delivered the advice that women should limit their drives to seventy or eighty yards: 'Not because we doubt a lady's powers to make a longer drive but because that cannot well be done without raising the club above the shoulder. Now we do not presume to dictate, but we must observe that the posture and gestures requisite for a full swing are not particularly graceful when the player is clad in female dress.'

'Their right to play, or rather the expediency of their playing the long round,' he continued, in a vein which would no doubt still receive an approving nod from many of today's male golfers, 'is much more doubtful. If they choose to play at times when the male golfers are feeding or resting, no one can object. But at other times, must we say it – they are in the way; just because gallantry forbids to treat them exactly as men.'

There were thirty-eight entries for that first British championship of 1893, with competitors homing in on St Anne's from as far afield as the Pyrenees and Portrush. It had been something of a toss-up as to whether the event should be played at the Wimbledon Club, where all the discussions about a prospective LGU had been taking place, or at St Anne's. In April of that year, the St Anne's members had announced in print that they had approved the purchase of a fifty-guinea challenge cup for an open competition.

As Enid Wilson, the former triple British champion and *Daily Telegraph* women's golf correspondent wrote in her *Gallery of Women Golfers*: 'The logical thing was for both parties to unite and this they did most amicably as soon as they became aware of each other's designs. Other clubs signified their willingness to co-operate in a practical manner by subscribing towards the trophy. Wimbledon, St Anne's and St Andrews all subscribed ten guineas and other donations were forthcoming to the tune of three guineas from Ashdown, five from Blackheath and a guinea from Brighton.'

The title went to an Englishwoman by name of Lady Margaret Scott when she defeated Issette Pearson, the LGU's honorary secretary, by 7 and 5. The two met again in the following year's final at Littlestone. Then, in 1895, Lady Margaret won for the third year in a row when she beat Miss E. Lythgoe at Portrush. At that, Lady Margaret's father, Lord Eldon, observed that his daughter should be allowed to keep the trophy. His request was refused.

In Lady Margaret, who was eighteen years of age when she won her first British championship, there was no trace of the histrionics to which Hutchinson had alluded. The legendary Cecil Leitch who, shortly before her death in 1977, spoke with justifiable pride of the way in which she had met all but one of the winners of the British Women's championship, remembered Lady Margaret as 'a very gentle soul, a golfer with perfect manners on and off the course'.

Lady Margaret's golf bore testimony to the fact that she came from a golfing family. In a feature in a *Golf Illustrated* of 1899, the writer told how it was from her father and her brothers that Lady Margaret 'acquired that graceful yet powerful style which has been so immensely admired but unfortunately never successfully imitated'. All three of her brothers who, like her, had learned golf in the park surrounding the family home, knew what it was to play to scratch handicaps, with the Hon. Michael Scott renowned for his winning of the Amateur championship at a time when he was a fifty-five-year-old grandfather.

Andrew Kirkaldy, runner-up to Willie Park in the Open of 1889, marvelled at Lady Margaret's ability 'to drive her gutta 130 or 140 yards, always gracefully'.

At the request of her father, Kirkaldy would play with the promising youngster when she travelled to St Andrews on family holidays. Kirkaldy recalled how he would give Lady Margaret a stroke a hole. On those occasions he beat her, there would be an extra half-sovereign from Lord Eldon, usually accompanied by the words: 'So that you may not let her down lightly.'

May Hezlet, who won the British three times between 1899 and 1907, and whose family were no less steeped in golf than the Scotts, spoke, in the nicest sense, of how Lady Margaret looked the part. In a passage to put one in mind of Laura Davies's description of how Seve Ballesteros 'grips and re-grips his wedge, almost as if it were alive', Miss Hezlet noted, 'her manner of handling the clubs proved at once that she was a master of the game'.

What the golfers wore was all-important. Lady Margaret, for

Issette Pearson, the LGU's first Honorary Secretary

example, graced the inaugural championship in a magnificent white shirt tucked into a long, tweed, check skirt, the outfit drawing attention to her trim waist. It has often been said that the women were fashionable to the point of being uncomfortable, although some of the follow-throughs caught by the pioneer golfing photographers hardly suggest that the ladies' actions were curtailed by what they wore.

The atmosphere of the early championships had much in common with country house parties. Competitors would enjoy musical evenings at the end of a day's golf while, on the Sunday, members of the host club

16

would invariably whisk them off, in horse-drawn carriages, on sightseeing tours.

In keeping with all of this, the first international match, a hastily thrown-together affair in which England defeated Ireland at Portrush on the day after the 1895 British championship, scarcely served as a blueprint for today's Home Internationals. That is if we are to believe what Mabel E. Stringer had to say: 'A dance had been given the night before, which was kept up till daylight, so Miss Pearson, who captained the English team, had, I remember, some little trouble in getting the players on to the tee at the scheduled time.'

Yet, in spite of the socialising, one suspects that, even in the championship's earliest years, there were plenty of golfers to whom a good performance in the event itself was almost everything.

Lady Margaret, in common with the other medalists at Portrush, had preferred not to get involved with that less-than-serious Anglo-Irish contest. Again, her rounds with Andrew Kirkaldy would even today be seen as just about the best form of match practice a player could have.

Just as Lady Margaret's steadfast and skilful performance from 1883

Competitors at Royal Portrush for the 1895 British Championship

to 1885 was exactly what was needed to make Horace Hutchinson retract his words, so the LGU was blessed with an outstanding official in Miss Pearson. A member of the Wimbledon Club, Miss Pearson and her golfing friends had been occupying their minds with such things as a standard handicapping system since the 1880s. She founded the Union in 1893 and gave generously of her time until the 1920s.

They did not come tougher than Miss Pearson. Born at Gatcombe House at Totnes in Devon in 1861, she moved with her family to Birkenhead in 1864 after Thomas Pearson, her father, had lost £10,000 or almost all his legacy in a bad investment. The loss stung him into action and, at the age of forty and with little or no previous business experience, he set about founding the insurance business upon which the family fortune was destined to be based.

Having organised a successful Liverpool office, he proceeded to London where Issette started her golf on Barnes Common. She ruled the roost here. Later, she sent journalists packing from a British final and, in so doing, became labelled 'as despotic as the Czar of Russia'. According to her nephew, David Pearson, who lives in Parkgate, South Wirral, she was

Lady Margaret Scott (right) on her way to defeating Amy Pascoe in the 1895 British Championship at Royal Portrush. Miss Pascoe won the championship the following year

Issette Pearson, the first Honorary Secretary of the LGU

'a considerable hazard to all and sundry who happened to be enjoying a walk'.

To her family's surprise, this seemingly established spinster would marry twice when she was over fifty. Her first husband was Tommy Miller, who, along with his first wife, Belle, had been a founder member of the Lytham and St Anne's Golf Club. Then, on Tommy's death, she became attached to a vicar by name of Thomas Herman, who was half her age.

This second liaison furnished golfers with the kind of gossip that stood the test of time. Issette, whose LGU rules and regulations people broke at their peril, tolerated a man of the cloth who would sire seven illegitimate children.

The team bus, 1906

'Formidable but kind,' is how Issette was seen by the surviving members of the Pearson family, while it was no less an authority than May Hezlet who, as early as 1904, penned the following tribute:

'The Union without Miss Pearson in her post of Hon Secretary would be a miserable institution, and it is mainly through her efforts and strong personality that it has gained its present flourishing condition. The post of Hon. Secretary to the LGU is no sinecure, but Miss Pearson is fully fitted to cope with the work, and succeeds in filling the responsible position in the most capable manner possible.' After further references to her 'tact and courtesy', Miss Hezlet went on to talk of Miss Pearson's undeniable skill as a golfer.

It is a measure of the lasting esteem in which she is held that, for as long as the GPO's old telegraphic system prevailed, the first line of the LGU code was an evocative 'Issette'.

RULES OF THE LGU AS LAID DOWN IN 1893

The Rules of the game shall be those published in 1892 by the R & A GC of St Andrews and shall be known by the Union as the Rules of the Game of the Ladies' Golf Union.

1) *To promote the interests of the game of golf*
2) *To obtain a uniformity of the rules of the game by establishing a representative legislative authority*
3) *To establish an uniform system of handicapping*
4) *To act as a tribunal and court of reference on points of uncertainty*
5) *To arrange the Annual Championship Competition and obtain funds necessary for that purpose.*

Miss Golf, Great Britain
Doris Chambers (1883–1983)
by Enid Wilson

If the Post Office found in their mail a letter addressed to 'Miss Golf, Great Britain', there would be no delay in transit, for it would go directly to Putney, where it would be delivered at the flat of Miss Doris Chambers.

Miss Chambers is known in every country where women play golf. She has travelled extensively, and for many years has taken great delight in looking after golfing visitors from overseas.

At all hours of the twenty-four she has been waiting to welcome teams and individuals, and her vigils have been kept at airports, landing stages and railway stations. For a long time she did this unofficially, but latterly she has been down in the *Handbook of the Ladies' Golf Unions and Clubs*.

This work consists of seeing that visitors at the British championship and other Open competitions are looked after, housed, fed, entertained and given all the golf they require.

Miss Chambers carries on a terrific correspondence, keeping in touch with all the people she has met, and through it she knows the results of competitions all over the world. The amount of information she gleans would suffice to keep a sports agency in business.

She has always taken a tremendous interest in juniors and there is not a golfer of note who has failed to receive from her congratulations and messages of encouragement from the time when they came to the fore in county golf. Many young golfers have been taken by her to competitions that they could not otherwise have played in, and her flat in London has been an open house for them when they wanted to stay in town.

The trophies, cups, medals and other prizes she has given away are countless. Cheshire has the 'Doris Chambers' Foursomes, the associations have several of her cups, and so have the South Eastern Division and Middlesex.

Few details of the administration of the LGU have escaped her

Doris Chambers

knowledge, for she has been in the closest possible contact with its work for something like forty years.

When the first touring team was sent abroad in 1933, to South Africa, Miss Chambers was an automatic choice as captain. Three of our touring teams – those of 1934, 1936 and 1948 – were captained by her, and in each of these her opposite number was Mrs E. H. Vare, better known as Miss Glenna Collett.

Miss Chambers has given so much to the game and to those who play it, that many people, especially the younger generation, are incapable of regarding her in any other capacity than that of benefactor.

Her home was Birkenhead and her club Wirral Ladies, one of the few courses in the country owned and maintained by women. With Mrs Temple Dobell and Mrs Allan Macbeth, Miss Chambers formed a Cheshire county triumvirate who were all British champions. In 1923 she won the British at Burnham and Berrow, beating Mrs Macbeth in the final.

Motoring has always been one of her main interests and she used to overhaul and service her own cars. The blue Vauxhall Velox tourer and the big, green Packard saloon were familiar to all who attended championships. In both wars Miss Chambers served with the FANY and during the 1914–1918 war she drove an ambulance in France.

When she moved south, Middlesex were after her immediately, and she has done a great deal for the county of her adoption, without ever ceasing to follow the fortunes of Cheshire.

It was inevitable that, with her quick wit and rapid movement, her swing was fast, too. Like George Duncan she played at the gallop and hit the ball hard and with exceeding crispness. Her strength and power brought her through the championship at Burnham, which is one of the longest and most exacting links used by women for their big tournaments. Her British was played through one of the stormiest championship weeks on record. Afterwards she was considerably amused to read the reports, for in some papers she was described as a promising young golfer and in others as 'the Cheshire veteran'.

In the 1960 New Year's Honours, Miss Chambers received a very well-deserved OBE and two months later was made President of the LGU.

from A Gallery of Women Golfers, 1961

CHAPTER TWO

Ireland's Golden Years

The Irish may well have had political and economic problems at the turn of the twentieth century, but nothing could have been more healthy over that period than the state of their women's golf. In the twelve years from 1899 to 1911, there was Irish involvement in nine finals of the British Women's championship, with no fewer than five Irish victories.

This extraordinary Irish supremacy had its origins in 1895 when the British championship, in what was only its third year, was held at Portrush. Miss Clara Mulligan, Ireland's answer to the LGU's Issette Pearson, had by all accounts been largely responsible for the coup.

May Hezlet poised to drive over the dunes

'Up until then,' to quote from *Ladies Golf*, published in 1904, 'the majority of Irish ladies had not thought or cared very much about golf, but with the advent of the Saxons from over the water a different aspect of the game was presented. They had not realised what a vast amount of skill could be achieved; the play of the strangers was a revelation, they were so keen and capable.

'From that time the Irish girls determined to apply themselves in deadly earnest to the science of the game, until they were able to maintain a complete mastery of the details, and so be enabled to hold their own against all-comers.'

No one was to prove more inspired than the writer, May Hezlet. She and Rhona Adair, who had been cleaning up in the junior and senior events at Portrush since they were eleven and twelve, had been unable to tear themselves away from the club when the top golfers were in town, their appetites having been whetted during the previous week's Irish Women's championship which had been won by a Miss Cox, the honorary secretary of the ladies' club at Portrush.

The atmosphere over the fortnight was captured in the pages of *The Sportswoman's Library*, published in 1898: 'The bustle and excitement in the streets of the little town was great, and outside cars came tearing round the perilously sharp corners, laden with red-coated golfers either off to watch the semi-finals of the Irish Ladies, or else to sample the truly grand course on their own account. Every train, too, brought in fresh relays of competitors, till the huge Northern Counties Hotel had not a corner untenanted.'

The two girls had teed up in the championships and thirteen-year-old Rhona, the daughter of the club captain, won the handicap award in a medal event open to all contestants at the British.

Five years on and the Misses Hezlet and Adair had each won the coveted British title. May bagged the trophy for a first time in 1899 at Newcastle County Down. Rhona, who was to win twice to May's thrice, followed suit the following summer at Westward Ho!

'Miss May', as she was affectionately known, began in May 1899 by winning the Irish championship at Newcastle. She celebrated her seventeenth birthday over the weekend and, the following week, completed a famous fortnight by collecting her British title over the same course. To this day, there has been no younger champion of the LGU's premier event.

The match between Miss Hezlet and Miss Adair in the final of the Irish was a fascinating affair. The gallery had pondered on how these two youngsters would cope with the mental strain of thirty-six holes, while they were no less occupied with the vexed question as to whether it was a coincidence that the girls hailed from the same place. 'The two opponents,' recalled Mabel Stringer in *Golfing Reminiscences*, penned in 1924, 'were very much of an age, their golf was fine and free, but at the same time well considered, and much more finished than that played by girls of a similar age nowadays.'

Rhona was not at her best in the morning, lunching four down but, in the afternoon, holes were ever more excitingly exchanged before 'Miss May' bagged her title.

Though the same may be applied to Rhona, May was quite accustomed to playing thirty-six holes in the one day. Even now, there are those at Portrush who can remember listening to May and her sisters, Emmie, Violet and Florence, talk of the days when they would cycle up to the course and play morning and afternoon before riding home. Zara Bolton, a runner-up in the English championship of 1948 and an erstwhile Curtis Cup player who has spent much of her life in Portrush, notes that the distance involved was a round trip of twenty-four miles over roads which were scarcely tarmacadam.

May once told Mrs Bolton how the family fervour was such that they would all chip and putt in the garden and how, when the Irish championship of 1908 was held at Portrush, all four sisters and their mother were in the draw, with May, Violet and Florence making the semi-finals before May defeated Florence by five and four in the final. Florence's

May Hezlet's full and free follow-through as demonstrated during the course of her win in the 1899 British Ladies' Championship at Newcastle County Down

Violet Hezlet

silver medal was one of nine runner-up medals collected by her, Emmie and Violet from the British and Irish championships.

May won three British and five Irish titles before she married the Reverend A. E. Ross, a gentleman who was to become the Bishop of Tuam and who, no doubt by way of ensuring that he could see rather more of his wife, lent his name to a petition that there should be no golf at Portrush on Sundays.

To mark the occasion of her marriage in 1909, the club presented May, whose handicap had at one point reached plus seven, with a Sheraton grand-father clock, an inlaid Sheraton corner cabinet and a massive silver salver.

In time, the couple moved to England and May dropped out of the championship scene to concentrate on being a minister's wife, though she would never lose interest in the goings-on at Portrush. She paid frequent visits to Ireland and, on the death of her husband, returned to live in the family home. Though childless herself, she was President of the Mother's Union and, at the same time, active for the WVS in the Portrush area. She also regularly attended committee meetings up at the golf club and eventually became the club's first president, a role in which her successor was none other than Rhona Adair.

In her seventies, 'Miss May' was once spotted on the links of the

Dunluce course. It was a haunting spectacle. She was on her own, knocking a few balls about and presumably, like Sir Bedevere, 'revolving many memories'.

The Hezlet family served their country well. . . .Mrs Hezlet had shown the way, playing in the first, informal international against the English in 1885. In 1901, both Mrs Hezlet and May won their matches as Ireland defeated the English to the tune of 5 to 2 in an unofficial international. In 1905, after considerable discussion between the Hezlet and Curtis sisters, May and Florence played at Cromer in a match against the Americans which was a forerunner of the Curtis Cup. Then, in 1907, all three of May, Violet and Florence were in the Irish side which became the first Irish team, men's or women's, to win an official international contest. They were presented with the same Miller Shield that is played for today, the trophy having been given to the women by Mr T. H. Miller, who would marry Issette Pearson and become a president of the LGU.

May's brother, Charles, not only represented Ireland but Great Britain and Ireland in the Walker Cup, while Emmie, who lost to Rhona Adair in the final of the 1900 Irish championship at Portrush, was another to don her country's colours, if only on an unofficial basis.

In that 1900 championship, Miss Adair had first to beat May in the semi-finals. She was three up at the turn, but square as she mounted the eighteenth tee. May later wrote of how 'a terrific squall came on at that moment, but the excitement was so intense that no one thought of waiting until it was over. Hats and umbrellas were gaily floating all over the course, the distracted owners pursuing their property in all directions.'

Fatally, 'Miss May' bunkered her drive at the last and Miss Adair found herself teeing up against the next Hezlet. Emmie stayed with her illustrious opponent over the morning instalment of the thirty-six hole final and was only one to the bad. But after lunch, as her sister recalled, she was, 'worn out with the wind and went completely off her game. Miss Adair, playing excellent golf, scored an easy victory.'

The second of Miss Adair's four successive Irish titles was won at Portmarnock in the days when the course was not linked to the mainland by road. The difficulty of access was something of a talking point: 'At high tide,' explained May, 'quite a long stretch of water has to be negotiated. . . . Some of the lady golfers did not at all relish the short sea voyage before playing and were very thankful when landed safely on terra firma.'

Miss Adair's next win was at Newcastle, and the fourth – and last – at Portrush when she defeated 'Miss May' in the semi-finals and sister Violet in the final.

'Miss Adair,' wrote May, with a generosity which was entirely in keeping with her character, 'is the most consistently good lady golfer in the world; others may equal her in brilliancy occasionally, but no one has the same wonderful power of always being on form. Her nerve and courage can ever be depended upon, and she shows to the best advantage at a critical moment. There seems to be an inexhaustible fund of reserve power ready to be drawn upon.'

May marvelled at how, on top of her major titles, Miss Adair had won a steady stream of minor competitions:

> Her silver table is a sight worth seeing. The majority of these trophies were won in scratch competitions and consist of beautiful silver bowls and cups, bon bon dishes, candlesticks etc etc. During her recent trip to America, Rhona carried off sixteen trophies from the different links she visited, some of them beautiful silver prizes and these find an honoured place on her table.
>
> Her trip was certainly a wonderful success. Only once during the whole time she was there was she defeated by an American lady golfer and when the fact is taken into consideration that she was in a strange land and climate and playing each day on strange links, after a deal of travelling and rushing about, her uniform success appears something marvellous. No other lady golfer in the world could have performed such wonders or given the American people such a splendid exhibition of fine play. The visit made a tremendous sensation over the water and will probably have the effect of arousing fresh interest in the game of golf and enlisting many new members into the already large ranks of enthusiasts.

Harold Hilton, when asked to comment on Miss Adair's swing, felt it necessary to prefix his analysis with the comment: '. . . the dictates of fashion preclude a sufficiently close diagnosis of methods. Miss Adair,' he none the less ventured, 'stands up to the ball in a manner quite worthy of any of the sterner sex. There is a determination and firmness in her address to the ball which is most fascinating to watch. Lady players, as a rule, appear to persuade the ball on its way; Miss Adair, on the contrary, avoids any such constrictions on her methods by hitting very hard indeed.'

'In addressing with an iron club,' he continued, 'it will be seen that Miss Adair follows the masculine precedent as she stands much more forward to the ball with the balance more on the left foot. At the top of the swing the club reaches an almost ideal position, showing clearly both command and freedom.'

He went on to liken her 'ease and elegance' at the top and finish of her swing to that favoured by the Hon. Osmund Scott, brother of Lady Margaret Scott. 'Miss Adair,' he concluded, 'holds the right hand well under, and I have an idea that she bends the left knee in considerably more than the average golfer. But this,' he added, in a lighthearted reference to her long skirt, 'is mere deduction!'

Hilton's stated suspicion that she had shortened her backswing was supported by May Hezlet: 'Within the last couple of years, her swing has altered, and at present is not nearly such a full one as formerly.' She added that a peculiarity about Miss Adair's style was that she used exceedingly short clubs, and held them 'well down the leather'.

Though May, with her classic swing and reputation for being 'the most finished golfer, man or woman, of the day', hit the ball a useful distance, Rhona was always the longer. When, for instance, both were invited to the Royal Lytham and St Anne's Ladies' Open Meeting in April, 1900, to celebrate the arrival of the twentieth century, Miss Adair won a long-driving contest with 'a fine rasper of 173 yards'. According to an editorial in *The Irish Golfer*, she was as much as twenty yards past her rivals.

If her length never ceased to be a talking-point, there was also much talk about that occasion in 1899 when she played thirty-six holes with 'Old' Tom Morris at St Andrews. There is no record of what start she

The Irish Team, 1929

received from Old Tom that day. In truth, it is perfectly possible that they played level, for that much-loved son of St Andrews was by then in his seventy-ninth year. Be that as it may, Miss Adair won the first hole and was still one up after the two rounds. By the end, Old Tom was mighty grateful that the score was no worse, for he had been determined 'not to be licked by a lassie'.

The excellent centenary book produced by Royal Portrush tells how, in 1907, Rhona married Captain A. H. Cuthell of the West Yorkshire Regiment and was soon a mother of two. That she and May should have bowed out at much the same time left a seemingly irreparable void in the Irish game. 'No country,' wrote Mabel Stringer, 'has produced such a family of brilliant golfers as the Hezlets, and since the day when the three sisters and Rhona Adair were in their prime, Irish golf has never been the same.'

Miss Stringer, who died in 1958 at the age of eighty-nine, would have learned of Philomena Garvey's win in the British championship at Gleneagles in 1957, but was not around to see this legendary Irishwoman complete her extraordinary haul of fifteen Irish titles.

The owner of an interlocking grip and a strong pair of wrists, Miss Garvey possessed a control of the longer irons which knew few parallels in the Fifties. 'The ball goes off with a click and bites when it hits the green,' noted Enid Wilson in her *Gallery of Women Golfers*.

Miss Garvey, who once lived on the edge of County Louth but now resides in Dublin, concedes that she did indeed enjoy her irons. Introduced to the game by her older brother, Kevin, a single-handicap player who was to win the East of Ireland championship, Miss Garvey feels, today, that she benefited from being stretched from the start. 'It definitely helped that I played so much with men . . . You have to try to keep up with them.'

She made impressive use of a two iron, wielding it less from the fairway than off the tee at short holes: 'In seaside winds, the last thing I wanted was to send the ball soaring with a four or five wood.' But perhaps the strongest club in her bag was a concentration so intense that she would not even be aware of low-flying aircraft. That concentration was with her from the day she started to play and, at least in her opinion, had most to do with a fierce desire to win.

In tight matches she would get nervous but, so cool did she look, her opponents always had the uneasy feeling that there was nothing they could do to get her rattled.

'The more she wins, the more she is likely to win,' said Miss Wilson, in a reference to the growing sense of impending doom with which her opponents would mount the first tee in the Irish championship. Philomena, for her part, felt the pressures building up as she added to her store of Irish titles but had a theory that, if she could get past the first round, all would

Mary McKenna, the owner of a record nine Curtis Cup caps

be well. Once through to the second round, she would relax somewhat, having the feeling that she was 'safely into the thick of things'.

Miss Garvey represented Ireland in the Home Internationals on no fewer than sixteen occasions and further played on six Curtis Cup sides. In the context of the former, her record was outstanding. Where the latter was concerned, she has always felt that she never came up with her best golf. Not the most outgoing of players, she will tell you that she seldom felt comfortable against American opposition. 'I never,' she explained, 'could get over the way they would shout such things as "Come on, Honey," to their golf ball. I tried not to let it bother me but it was not my style and difficult to take.'

Having said as much, Miss Garvey admitted that she had got on

Maisie Mooney (left) and Jane Lock after Maisie had set the 1973 Australian title alongside the Irish Championship of that year. Having emigrated to Australia the Irish player now holds a senior post on the Australian Ladies' Golf Union

Lillian Behan (left), British Champion in 1985 and a long hitter whose strong arms owe much to her years as a stable girl at the Curragh

splendidly with the greatest extrovert of them all, Babe Zaharias. They met in a match between the American professionals and British amateurs in the early Fifties at Sunningdale Ladies'. The match was supposed to be over eighteen holes and it is not too difficult to imagine how the Irish player must have felt when, after she had finished the round two holes to the good, she was told of a decision to make the matches thirty-six hole affairs.

Ultimately, Miss Zaharias won at the thirty-sixth having, at that last hole, arrived beside the flag with a shot which cannoned first off a tree and then the clubhouse wall.

Though the scale of Philomena's achievements suggests that she was among those of her generation who could afford to play the game full-time, she was in fact busily employed in a Dublin store and able to pursue her golf only at weekends. Moreover, she was hampered by tender skin. In the week of a championship, her hands would be covered in blisters, these miniature water-hazards causing rather more trouble than the average opponent.

In recent years, Mary McKenna, who says that Philomena Garvey was positively worshipped by the golfing youth of her day, has enjoyed much the same golfing supremacy in her native land. Irish champion for the first time in 1969 and most recently in 1989, Mary, in among her eight Irish titles, has played in a record nine Curtis Cups. Recently, on celebrating twenty-one years at the top of the Irish amateur game, she was asked why her appetite for the game has remained unchanged.

Claire Hourihane, a five-times champion whose selection for the 1992 Curtis Cup at Hoylake increased her haul of Curtis Cup caps to four

'With each Curtis Cup,' she philosophised, 'one gathers more in the way of realisation that the Americans are not unbeatable – and this makes all the hard work that bit more appetising. I was lucky in that I played myself onto my first Curtis Cup side long before I knew or understood what the match was all about. Then, having played in it a few times, I started thinking in terms of records. There was first the ambition to match Jessie Valentine's record seven Curtis Cups. Then, when I matched that and then beat it, a new target presented itself – namely, one of matching Christy O'Connor's ten Ryder Cups and Joe Carr's ten Walker Cups.'

Another source of inspiration for Miss McKenna, whose game has benefited from having such strong Irish contemporaries as Maureen Madill, Lillian Behan and Claire Hourihane, all of whom have shone

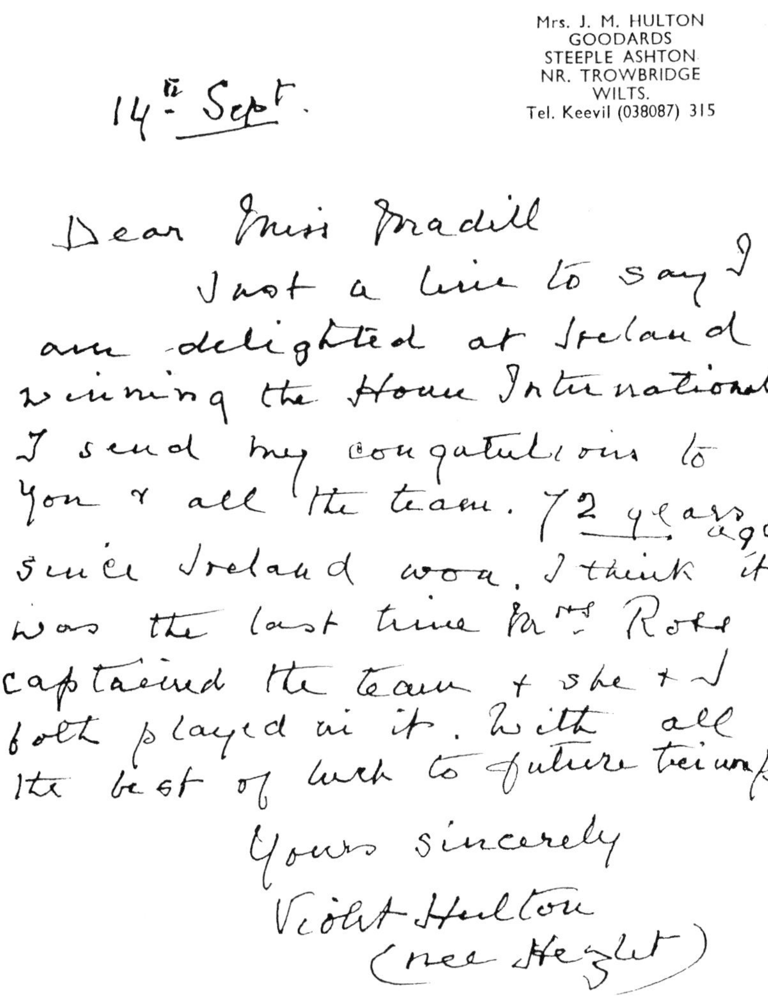

Mrs. J. M. HULTON
GOODARDS
STEEPLE ASHTON
NR. TROWBRIDGE
WILTS.
Tel. Keevil (038087) 315

14ᵗʰ Sept.

Dear Miss Madill

Just a line to say I am delighted at Ireland winning the Home Internationals I send my congratulations to you & all the team. 72 years ago since Ireland won. I think it was the last time Mrs Ross captained the team & she & I both played in it. With all the best of luck to future triumphs

Yours sincerely
Violet Hulton
(nee Hezlet)

Ireland's golden years: a letter from Violet Hulton, née Hezlet, to congratulate Maureen Madill on captaining Ireland to what was their first win in over 70 years in the Home Internationals

beyond the Emerald Isle, is that the swing she is using in the 1990s is better than the swing she owned in the preceding decades. For years, this most popular of Irish golfers knew that she could be more consistent. Which was why, when details emerged as to how Nick Faldo had been prepared to revamp his swing under the eye of David Leadbetter, she sought out this great teacher for herself.

Leadbetter agreed to coach her at Lake Nona during the winter of 1989–90 and when Mary, then forty, returned to the amateur circuit in

*Back row (left to right): Aideen Rogers, Nicola Gorman, Sandra Keane, Tricia Mangan,
Deirdre Powell Front row (left to right): Alison Coffey, Geraldine Doran, Michella
McGreevy*

1990, there was no mistaking the more professional outline to her swing. She just missed a place in the 1990 Curtis Cup side and was again unlucky in 1992 but, with the insatiable Anne Sander having played for America at the age of fifty-two, she knows that her goal of ten Curtis Cups is still on the cards.

No less impressive is the fact that she has represented her country in each of the biennial European Team championships since 1969. Ireland won that event in 1979 at the Hermitage – a result which, in conjunction with Maureen Garner's triumph in that year's British Match-Play championship at Nairn and Miss McKenna's own win in the Stroke-Play at Moseley, made the women the toast of their country. In 1983, they won the European Team championships again, this time at Royal Waterloo in Belgium.

In the context of the Home Internationals, Ireland have captured the coveted Miller Trophy only thrice – on that aforementioned occasion in 1907, and then in 1980 and 1986. The first two wins may have been in two very different eras, but they were linked by a note which is among Maureen Garner's most treasured possessions.

It came from one Violet Hulton of Trowbridge who, in congratulating Miss Madill, as she was then, and her team, pointed to how she had been a member of the Ireland side on the occasion of their last win, 'seventy-two years ago'.

Violet Hulton, as you will have guessed, was none other than Violet Hezlet.

Golfers Aglow, 1930

To avoid chills

The best preventative for colds is a hot footbath immediately after each game. Alternatively, rub feet with methylated spirits or Eau-de-Cologne. Massage until warm glow felt from heels to toes.

Slimming

Add an ounce of Epsom Salts to the daily bath and once a week make an extra strong solution by using four to eight ounces.

Wrong Lines

The chief danger for the woman golfer who wants to preserve her looks is the harm which she unconsciously does to her expression. This, of course, is caused simply and solely by the tremendous concentration which is required during play – and a general anxiety to do her best. . . .

It is terribly difficult to regulate one's features and keep them mask-like, but it is quite easy, with a little practice, to keep them serene in the face of bunkers and the like.

Frowns are devastating to beauty, while nervous twitching of the eyes is responsible for countless minute lines.

Lady Margaret Scott and the long but beautifully balanced swing with which she won the first three British Championships, 1893–1895

CHAPTER THREE

Golfing Dress

There was no shortage of criticism when women golfers first started wearing trousers. 'The end must justify the jeans,' was the mischievous verdict of Frank Moran, *The Scotsman*'s golf correspondent for sixty years. Much the same message was forthcoming from Moran's successor, who euphemistically deemed it a sphere in which 'some have bigger handicaps than others'.

With nineteenth-century jokes about women golfers no doubt running along much the same lines as those of today, it was hardly surprising that, back in 1899, a leading player of the day, Miss M. Boys, in *Our Lady of the Green*, should have poured scorn on that element who were to be seen sporting 'soft hunting ties, loose red shapeless coats, and the shortest and narrowest of bicycling skirts'.

The lovely May Hezlet wasted no time in letting it be known that she shared Miss Boys's concern. 'Anything,' she wrote, 'that makes the wearer conspicuous is out of place on the links. Outrageous or indifferent dressing raises remarks about "athletic women". We must prevent disparaging remarks which are too apt to be made after a ladies' golf meeting . . . The aim of all lady golfers of the present day must be to abolish the absurd but popular belief, which must have started somewhere, that "a golfing girl" is a weird and terrible creature clad in the most extraordinary garments, striding along with self-possessed walk, and oblivious to everything but her beloved game.'

Miss Boys's idea of what the woman golfer of the day should be wearing was as follows: 'A neat sailor-hat, surmounting a head beautifully coiffured, every hair of which is in its place at the end of a round. A smart red coat, a spotless linen collar and tie, an ordinary tailor-made skirt, and a pair of well-made walking-boots with nails of Scafe's patent soles.'

One can only assume that the players sporting those outfits of which Miss Boys and Miss Hezlet so disapproved were subtly shepherded into the back rows of the earliest group photographs for, to the casual observer, the pictures recording the first years of the British Women's championship suggest untold elegance.

The ladies would take up positions to show themselves and their outfits to best advantage, while the effect of casual grace was enhanced by the introduction of the odd golf club. Yet some are insistent that these fashion-conscious souls paid dearly in terms of comfort. Though such as Miss Hezlet and her great rival, Rhona Adair, no doubt escaped such torture on account of their youth, the average woman golfer was by all accounts encased in corsets replete with whale bones and lacing.

'Having constricted their middles,' relates Enid Wilson, in her *Gallery of Women Golfers*, 'the ladies then proceeded to add drapes, such as puff sleeves and voluminous skirts.' The women further wore boaters and buttoned boots and, rather like horses in a handicap chase, the best of them were apt to be weighed down with medals won in open meetings and the like.

High, stiff collars – and club ties – were 'another part of the uniform', while strips of leather were sewn on to the bottom of a skirt in order to prevent fraying. Then there was 'a Miss Higgins', an elastic band named after an ingenious American lady, a Miss M. B. Higgins. This would be slipped over the skirt's folds in order to keep the garment contained in winds such as Miss Higgins no doubt faced on that day in 1904 when, in losing to Rhona Adair in the first round of the British Women's champion-ship at Troon, she was referred to in the press as 'America's plucky representative'.

So convinced was the legendary Joyce Wethered that such outfits stopped their wearers from being seen at their best, at least in the golfing sense, that she maintained that changing fashions after the war contributed vastly to the sudden advance in the women's game.

Not that the fashions of her day were everything they might have been. For example, in the English championship of 1924 at Cooden Beach in the Pevensey Marshes, one knitted skirt became so saturated with rain that its occupant could no longer move. With the match still all square as she ground to a halt at the eighteenth, the competitor sought help from officialdom.

She asked if she might repair to the clubhouse and put her skirt through a mangle or, alternatively, slip into another garment. Though there was no known precedent, the LGU gave their blessing to the donning of a new skirt. According to Mabel Stringer, the lady in question succeeded in shaking off her opponent at the nineteenth.

It was forty-eight years after she had won her last British title that Lady Amory realised what might have been on the clothing front. Namely, when she accepted an invitation to watch the women professionals in action at the Women's Masters at Hilton Head. At that point, it was not merely as golfers that the US women professionals were out on their own. Their pastel, mix-and-match outfits were light years removed from anything on offer in the professionals' shops on this side of the Atlantic.

'I just wish,' said Lady Amory, on her return, 'that trousers had been in vogue in my day as skirts were such a problem. They would fall just above the ankle and you had to be very careful that they were tight enough not to flap, yet loose enough to let you take up your stance. Trousers apart, the only practical garment has to be a short skirt such as the Americans now wear.'

The first player to wear trousers in these islands was Gloria Minoprio, whose dramatic appearance at the English championship of 1933 has its own special niche in the lore of British women's golf.

Others wasted no time in following suit but, where many looked no less striking than Miss Minoprio, others saw trousers as the easy way out and standards tended to slip. All over the country clubs introduced rules stating, often a little ambiguously, that women should remove their slacks before entering the lounge.

One player who did as much as anyone to sharpen on-course fashion instincts in these islands was Marley Spearman, British champion in 1961 and 1962. Marley was a dancer who, when she turned to golf at the age of twenty-six, could not, for the life of her, understand the way in which golfers would prepare for their sport. She would watch, spellbound, as this strange breed would produce from their lockers worn and seated tweed skirts with a statutory pleat at the back, these to be accompanied by crumpled tops, usually waterproof, which had similarly seen better days.

'I could never comprehend why all this was necessary,' she once said. 'After all,' she continued, cheerfully oblivious to those of golf's starters who spend their time rummaging for lost balls in burns and briers, 'it's not like gardening . . . you aren't likely to get muddy or anything.'

Marley, it was said, was as colour television is to black and white. She had exquisite taste and, from the start, saw the golf course as an excellent platform for sporting the latest fashions. Later, when she moved into the international arena, what Marley wore was always a matter of pressing interest to her followers – and there is a story, maybe apocryphal, of how, when fire broke out in the Bell Hotel in Barnby, the cry went up 'Save Marley's clothes'.

The LGU are justifiably proud of the team uniforms they produce for the Great Britain and Ireland side for the Curtis Cup. In truth, the kitting out of the eight players must rank as one of the most difficult tasks on the agenda. It is always difficult to please everyone, but the LGU have yet to find themselves in the same situation as did Sue Mappin, the LTA's director of women's tennis, when she got the thumbs down from every member of one junior international side.

Remembering how excited she had felt on that day, not too many years before, when she had unpacked her first international track suit, Miss Mappin had waited, with baited breath, for the youngsters' reactions. As

Joyce Wethered

it turned out, there was a long and deathly hush before one among them put thoughts into words.

'Flared trousers,' came the succinctly damning and disgusted exclamation.

The rules prevailing at tournaments run under the LGU umbrella ask that players should not wear 'short shorts, jeans, trainers or sun-tops'. The instruction appears on most entry forms, including that of the Helen Holm trophy, an event played in April at Troon. In this latter instance, it should, if nothing else, serve successfully to confuse the European contingent in the matter of what they should be packing for their early-season Scottish weekend.

Jeans, though very much *de rigueur* in Continental clubs, are frowned upon in Britain – and totally forbidden on the women's professional circuit. Most are *au fait* with the story of how the women professionals' in-house rule was broken by Laura Davies just two weeks after she had turned professional. The Surrey golfer was not wearing jeans as such but, to the then director of the Women's European Tour, any garment which hinted of denim was as a red rag to a bull.

Miss Davies, though she finished second behind Jan Stephenson in what was only her second professional tournament, was genuinely upset at being labelled 'scruffy', not least because she at that stage had no money to spend on a new wardrobe.

The sponsor, Giles Hennessy, sprang to her defence. 'Laura looked all right to me', said he, protectively. As for Miss Stephenson, she made the point that the powers-that-be would have been better employed feeling proud of Miss Davies at such a moment.

The English player was duly fined £50, but the repercussions as far as officialdom was concerned were such that Joe Flanagan, when he became Executive Director, wisely vowed never to get involved in that side of things.

A more recent example of appearances scoring over play, at least in the national press, came at the start of 1990. Two American professionals, Deborah McHaffie and Tammie Green, were the delighted, if surprised, recipients of appearance money at the Hennessy tournament in France. Though they did not know it until the press revealed as much, the two of them had been chosen less for their golf than their looks. The pair's stance over the issue was disarming: 'If we've been chosen for our looks we're flattered.'

Their sister competitors similarly took the news with humour rather than rancour. Indeed, though it was hardly the reaction the feminists would have wanted, at least ninety per cent came up with a 'good for them', or something along those lines.

It goes without saying that the whole business inspired many a cartoon back home. Of them all, pride of place went to that depicting the starter at a women's open meeting telling a motley crew of competitors, 'I can assure you, ladies, none of you were asked here for your looks!'

From *Taylor on Golf*

The best of the lady golfers were naturally to be found in the ranks of those who were fortunate enough to be able to learn the game during the days of their childhood; and as I said in respect of a man, the earlier in life you can commence playing golf, so much the better chance do you possess of coming to the front.

Ladies whose homes are in Scotland have this great advantage over all other competitors. Golf has been played over the Border to a far greater extent than here in England, and at the present time it would be possible, perhaps, to select a team of lady golfers, members of the various Scottish clubs, who would defeat any other similar team in the world. But with the rapid advance of the game in the south of England the standard of play must necessarily become high, until, in a few years, our English ladies should reach a similar pitch of excellence.

J. H. TAYLOR, 1902

Laura Davies

From Round Scotland – A Scottish Introduction *By Lady Heathcoat-Amory*

Everyone, including Doctor Johnson, must have recognised the distinction between the road leading out of Scotland and the one leading into it. No one appreciates the difference in emotion when pursuing those opposing routes more than I do. For the last ten years or so I have been an inveterate visitor to this neighbouring country; and although I cannot claim a drop of Scottish blood in my veins, I own to a feeling of absolute content whenever I cross the border. . . .

One reason, though not by any means the only reason, why I love Scotland, is perhaps the unworthy one that I feel I play better there than anywhere else. That is an inducement that no golfer can resist. A course or an atmosphere that encourages one to play well, and flatters one's game, is a place to hurry to at all costs. . . .

ST ANDREWS

What a joy it is to jump into the train in the evening at a London terminus, with one's clubs on the rack overhead, and to wake the next morning to the sounds of Edinburgh and then the strange hum of the train rumbling over the Forth Bridge. A few battleships lie quiet and still far beneath, dull shapes in the hazy morning light which is slowly uncovering the stretches of the Firth and the little groups of houses clustered along the shore.

It is a journey as full of charm and interest as the destination for which we are bound. The last mile or so runs down the side of the links and the first exciting glimpse of St Andrews is caught. . . .

The University rises an impressive pile of buildings in the very heart of the town. Students provide an effective note of colour in their bright scarlet gowns, whether in the dark grey streets, or when mingling in a gallery on the links against the dull green background. Nor are the more juvenile scholars forgotten. They may be seen in scattered groups on

Sundays, invading the empty course and the sands on their afternoon walks. On the very big occasions they sometimes join the golfing galleries, peering, with apparent zeal at any rate, through openings provided by their elders. I can remember in the ladies' championship [the British Women's championship of 1929] being kept an embarrassed prisoner in the midst of a swarm of little dark blue-clad figures from St Leonards, flushed with the fever of autograph hunting and clutching stubbly pieces of pencil and odd bits of paper.

The older inhabitants of St Andrews may be indifferent and superior to autographs, but are all of them golfers bound together in one common enthusiasm for the game. It is talked of, thought of, practised by all. When I have stayed there, even in the shops I have found the same lively interest. The chemist hopes I am finding the course to my liking; the stationer asks me how I am playing; and the hairdresser to whom I have paid a hurried visit, is plainly more interested in my golf than in my coiffure.

It is useless to try to pretend that St Andrews appeals to everyone. To some it may appear cold and unattractive; the links may seem a flat and dreary expanse, with too many blind holes, hidden bunkers and bad lies. An unfortunate collection of faults to begin with, you might say!

To others St Andrews appeals in all the glory of its past history, a battlefield that has been the scene of countless victories and a course requiring a never-ending stock of intricate and cunning shots to defeat the broken quality of the ground . . . .

Driving from the first tee on the following morning, I remember I was not altogether free from terror. My knees were inclined to be unsteady; the tee seemed a vast and empty space, and my ball and myself very small and insignificant in the middle of it. To make things more disturbing still, the large plate glass window in the club room overlooking us was filled with faces. . . .

On a day's fishing in the Girvan which followed her win over Cecil Leitch at the 37th in the final of the 1925 British Women's Open at Troon . . .

It was in this river that I caught my first salmon. It happened to be a day or two after the exhausting final at Troon, and even then it appears I could not escape its dramatic associations. I was sent out alone with the keeper and we made our way to the most promising of swift-running pools, known as Donald's Wield. The very first time I cast down the pool I landed a twelve-pound salmon. Almost as soon as the fly was again in the water a second salmon seized it and made off. He was a keen fighter and beside his rapid and violent rushes he jigged and hoggled at the line so hard that my left arm, already weary after landing the other fish, and not used to this strenuous form of treatment, felt as if it would drop off at any moment.

I was also tired out from the golf of the previous week. After a quarter of an hour of playing the fish I cried out feebly that I could hold on no longer. The keeper was by this time creeping warily below the bank with his shining gaff prepared for action. Already excited by my 'beginner's luck', he urged me frantically not to give in. In a moment of final exhortation he shouted at me, 'Aye, and imagine it's Miss Leitch you've got hold of at the end of the hook!' So startled was I and so entertained by this grim picture (I was not even aware that he knew anything about golf) that I forgot my troubles and hung on as I was bid.

Whether or not my imagination was capable of rising to the occasion I cannot say; but at any rate in another five minutes the fish was landed and we gazed triumphantly on our prize on the bank. I could not help making a shrewd guess that, if Miss Leitch had been the fisherwoman, it was I who would have been for the gillie the unlucky salmon hooked and landed that day.

And so golf and fishing unite in one delightful memory to remind one of the pleasures which no place in the world can supply in the same ample measure as Scotland.

Golfing Memories and Memoirs, 1933

CHAPTER FOUR

Keep Right On to the End of the Road

SCOTS WHO BEAT THE YEARS

Old Tom Morris who was prevailed upon by competitors to make a speech at the 1903 Scottish Ladies' Championship at St Andrews. 'Old Tom' said that the ladies deserved 'very great credit' for their play

Charlotte Beddows, a semi-finalist in the Scottish Women's championship of 1905 at North Berwick, had a gleam in her eye as she swept round the side of the Longniddry clubhouse some seventy years later.

It was obvious that the visitor who enquired after her health was in no danger of being regaled with a litany of complaints. Indeed, Mrs Beddows bypassed matters medical altogether in her reply. 'I have,' she exclaimed, excitedly, 'added an extra fifteen yards to my tee shots.'

For the benefit of today's golfing octogenarians, one had best reveal that Mrs Beddows, who was born in 1887 and died in 1976, had been working on a piece of advice given to her by Gordon Durward, the late Longniddry professional. To wit, that she should keep her right elbow tucked in at the address.

The excitement she felt was not limited to her woods. At a time when her contemporaries were doing well to control their knitting needles, Mrs Beddows was still launching into her golfing irons in a manner to suggest that a seventh hole in one was just around the corner.

Hers was a life-long enthusiasm which contributed to a record in which she played for Scotland twenty-two times between 1913 and 1951 and represented East Lothian through six decades.

She also played for Great Britain and Ireland in the inaugural Curtis Cup, while she won four Scottish championships, together with an impressive array – seven to be precise – of silver and bronze medals. Talking of that haul, it was forty-five years after she had reached the semi-finals of the 1905 championship that, as a sixty-two-year-old, she played in the 1950 final at St Andrews. On that occasion, her opponent was a mere stripling of forty-three, Helen Holm.

It was no doubt in a bid to fit in still more golf that Mrs Beddows would play at an incredible rate of knots. 'Double-quick time', said Enid

Scotland Team at Burnham, 1906

Wilson, feelingly, for she had partnered the Scot in that 1932 Curtis Cup. The two had, in fact, reeled off some tremendous figures in losing, at the penultimate hole, to Virginia van Wie and Helen Hicks.

In keeping with her pace of play, Mrs Beddows did not beat around the proverbial bush when it came to speaking her mind. In which connection, there is the lovely tale of how she greeted Belle Robertson's apology for having kept her waiting a couple of times during the second qualifying round of a Scottish championship at Elie. 'I'm very sorry,' ventured Belle, who had been in the match directly in front, 'if I held you up.'

'My dear,' replied this grand old lady of Scottish golf, 'you didn't just hold me up, you held up the whole field!'

Though Mrs Beddows was wont to arrive at her golfing engagements in a chauffeur-driven Jaguar, she was the antithesis of soft. She was well over seventy when she dismissed out of hand the suggestion that she should install central heating in her home on Gullane Hill. No more did she feel the cold outside, setting forth for her daily fix of golf even on those days when the chilled rain was horizontal.

And when, in the Second World War, the condition of her beloved Gullane hit rock bottom, she organised working parties to handle weeding and bunker repairs until the course was as beautifully groomed as she was herself.

Elsie Grant-Suttie escapes the rushes and goes on to win the 1910 British Women's Championship at Westward Ho! The Scot, who was an ambulance driver in both World Wars, won her National Championship in 1911 and played six times in the Home Internationals

Jessie Valentine, six times a Scottish champion and the owner of one of the finest Curtis Cup records of all time (photograph by courtesy of The Scotsman*)*

Always she put back rather more than merely her divots, for no one could have done more to help East Lothian's juniors. 'She certainly encouraged me,' recalls Marjorie Ferguson who, as Marjorie Fowler, reached the final of the Scottish championship in 1966 and 1971.

'She expected you to walk smartly, not to dither when it came to club selection, and always to play the percentage shot,' said Mrs Ferguson. 'As youngsters,' she continued, 'we always used to feel very honoured if we were asked to play with Mrs Beddows or other Gullane luminaries such as Marjorie Draper and Jean Anderson. We did not get the coaching that young players have today and we saw games with these great players as a vital part of our golfing education.'

The 1929 Scotland team at St Andrews

There was one occasion when Mrs Beddows followed a game in which her young protegé ran up a comfortable lead, only to relax and let it dwindle. 'That,' said the experienced one, 'should teach you a lesson.' The reprimand was ringing in Marjorie's ears when, some time later, she had to play Mrs Beddows in the Scottish championship.

Of the two, Marjorie was the more grief-stricken when she defeated her elderly heroine on the tenth green. But, much though it tore at her heart, she knew that Mrs Beddows would have been down on her like a ton of bricks had she eased up and given her the odd hole.

Though Mrs Beddows's name is cited more than any other by those looking for evidence to support the oft-repeated theory that Scots enjoy a greater golfing longevity than their counterparts down south, there are many others. . . .The aforementioned Mrs Draper, for instance, reached the final of the Scottish championship and played for her country at the age of fifty-seven. Then again, there are the careers of such as Helen Holm, Jessie Valentine and Belle Robertson. . . .

When Mrs Holm defeated Mrs Beddows to take the 1950 Scottish championship, that represented her fifth and final win in the national championship. She had won for a first time at Turnberry in 1930 while, early on in that run, she collected the British championships of 1934 and 1938. Where the Curtis Cup was concerned, this imposing Troon golfer played in the matches of 1936, 1938 and 1948, but turned down an invitation to participate in an American-based Curtis Cup on the grounds that her son, Michael, was too young to be left.

Whereas Mrs Beddows's greatest strength lay in her pluck, Mrs Holm had about her a mental and physical toughness which were incomparable. In winning the second of her quintet of Scottish titles, she ultimately overcame one Miss M. G. Couper at the fifth extra hole. Another example of her great staying power manifested itself after she had had a thrombosis in the autumn of 1951.

Though the general feeling was that her golfing days were done, Helen Holm picked up four further medals in the Scottish championship, two of them silver. Not only that, but she was still, as Belle Robertson was not alone in discovering, an opponent to be feared in the Sixties. Belle, who owns to having learned from Mrs Holm 'what control and delicacy of touch are all about', came out on the losing side of their match in the 1960 Scottish championship at Turnberry: 'She [Mrs Holm] was none too fit and fifty-three years of age, but the sheer brilliance of her touch on a course which was that week dry and bouncy had to be seen to be believed.'

The putter, with which Mrs Holm went about her business, now does duty as the Helen Holm Trophy, an event which came into being two years after her death in 1971. It may be stroke-play rather than the match-play she knew rather better but, with two rounds over her beloved Troon Portland and the denouement over the Open championship links of Royal Troon, it each year draws much the same calibre of entry as does the British Stroke-Play. Belle Robertson and Wilma Aitken are the only players to have won three times apiece.

Helen Holm would have been proud of the event which bears her name.

Jessie Valentine's seemingly insatiable appetite for the game was captured by George Houghton in his entertaining book, *Golf Addict Among the Scots*.

'Within the world of women's golf,' wrote Houghton, 'she seems to have won everything: the British championship, three times; the Scottish championship, six times . . . . But the interesting part, at any rate to me, is that despite flogging around in major golf for nearly four decades, Jessie is still completely addicted to the game and doesn't mind admitting it.'

To Enid Wilson, Jessie Valentine has golf 'in her blood and in the marrow of her bones'.

Born in 1915, Jessie won her first British championship in 1937, her second in 1955 and her third in 1958. In other words, there was a twenty-one-year gap between her first win and her last – a feat which deservedly has its place in the *Guinness Book of Golf.*

It was snooker's Stephen Hendry who, in explaining why success had not gone to his head in the manner which had afflicted fellow players in the South, spoke of how 'There's none of this fame nonsense in Scotland. No one takes any notice of you.' Jessie's father, Joe, a teaching-professional-cum-clubmaker and a keen cricketer who opened the batting for Scotland, could have been said to have contributed to this state of affairs.

When, for example, his elated daughter came on the phone with news of how she had won the 1933 British Girls' championship, Joe's immediate retort, according to Houghton, was: 'You're not up to much if that's all you can win.'

And then there was the tale of that rain-lashed final day of the 1934 Scottish championship when Jessie asked of her father if she might have a pair of waterproof trousers. 'If ye canna win wi'oot breeks, y'll no win at a',' said he, unequivocally.

That Jessie's game was to last so well had most to do with the simple technique instilled in her by her father from the day she started as a five-year-old. Enid Wilson, for example, saw her as being 'very straightforward

The Curtis Cup team at Gleneagles, 1936. From left to right: Miss Wanda Morgan, Miss Jessie Anderson, Miss Phyllis Wade, Miss Bridget Newell, Miss Doris Chambers, Mrs Marjorie Garon, Mrs Helen Holm, Miss J. B. Walker, Miss Pam Barton

57

and orthodox in her methods' and as having only one mannerism. This was the transferring of her weight from one foot to the other several times. 'Not until the position and balance feels right does she start the club moving away into the backswing,' said Miss Wilson.

When she did start the backswing, her thought was one of brushing the turf at the take away 'for at least six inches'. But above all, as she has said in her book, *Better Golf Definitely*, Jessie Valentine believed in the importance of 'anchoring as opposed to locking' the head.

'At contact,' she wrote, 'the clubhead briefly stays with the ball. Rather than have this split-second feature disturbed, I always discipline myself not only to try to see the actual strike, but I keep watching until after the clean click of impact.

'I know that for the drive I will never see the clubhead actually strike the ball (although I shall continue to try), and, as for the click, the striker never hears it, because his concentration on staring at the ball and the lightning movement of the swinging club completely blot out all sense of hearing. But the click is felt. Then, and only then, should the head be allowed to ride round on the anchor.'

Playing seven times in the Curtis Cup, Jessie was in the winning teams of 1952 and 1956, besides sharing the halved matches of 1936 and 1958. The 1936 match was at Gleneagles. Jessie was the local girl and her performance in holing a huge putt across the last green to avert a British defeat is still talked of in those parts. Jean Anderson, the Scot with whom her career for so long went hand in hand, was another to feature on the winning side of 1952.

Besides amassing great records within and without Scotland, Jessie and Jean both turned professional and attached their maiden names to sets of clubs so popular that, in the Sixties, the golfer looking for new equipment had simply to choose between a set of Jessie Valentine's or Jean Donald's.

Another thing the two had in common was that both were left-handed but played golf right-handed. Jessie started the game with right-handed clubs that were lying around her father's shop and, in winning the world over, obviously never lost any sleep worrying as to whether she could be doing better the other way around. Mind you, after one particularly lean spell on the greens, she did try putting left-handed: 'It worked for a bit, but not for long.'

The only player in the 1948 Curtis Cup to win singles and four-somes, Jean Anderson was maybe more ambidextrous than a pure south-paw. 'I hoe the garden with my left hand, do my teeth right-handed and throw a ball left-handed,' explained Gullane's favourite daughter, who won the Scottish championships of 1947, 1949 and 1952.

It came as a great shock when Jean, aged sixty-six, died suddenly in

1981 after having been taken ill in Gullane's car-park. She had been preparing for an early-morning game with her friends, all of whom had been firmly under the impression that this staunch soul would be beating them for many years to come.

Jessie's love-affair with the game continues. . . . Awarded the MBE for her services to golf in 1959, and the Frank Moran Trophy in 1967, she played no small part in the destiny of the British Stroke-Play trophy of 1986. With that year's championship being staged at Blairgowrie, she offered to caddie for Claire Hourihane, an Irish player in the same beautifully organised mould as she herself. Level with England's Trish Johnson after four rounds, Miss Hourihane won at the first extra hole and, in so doing, paid a moving tribute to the Scot at her side.

Another player in Claire's age group who has similarly benefited from Jessie's experience is Gillian Stewart. Gillian was not vaguely surprised at Jessie's lovely, lazy backswing, but she was in for a shock when her septuagenarian opponent followed through. 'It was a far more aggressive follow-through than the one I'd expected,' confessed the Inverness golfer.

One piece of advice which stayed with Gillian concerned how to get by on a day when she was feeling jaded. 'When you're tired,' recommended Jessie, 'give it your tired swing. Don't ask your body to do more than it feels like doing.'

It is not uncommon, at club level, for a junior skidding down the handicap charts to capture most of the trophies. In 1991, it was one Joan Barrie Lawrence who cleaned up at Dunfermline's annual awards dinner. However, far from being a junior, Joan was at that point sixty-one years of age. . . .

Winner of the Scottish championship in 1962, 1963 and 1964 and a finalist the following year when she lost to Belle Robertson, Joan played as a Scottish international between 1959 and 1970 besides playing in the Curtis Cup of 1964. Her short game was grimly relentless, with none among her peers able to match her ability to get down in two from a hundred yards.

An international selector between 1973 and 1976 and again from 1980 to 1983, she went on to become a most effective chairman of the LGU in 1989.

What with a full-time job and her many LGU commitments, Joan found her golf suffering, with her once plus-two handicap going up to four. Which was why, on her more-or-less concurrent retirement from work and the LGU, she decided to get back in the swing of things on the golfing front.

The highlight of the sexagenarian Miss Lawrence's 1991 season, a season in which she returned to two in the handicap stakes, was a brace of 70s against the par of 72 at her home course.

> *And children coming home from school*
> *Look in at the open door;*
> *They love to see the flaming forge,*
> *And hear the bellows roar,*
> *And catch the burning sparks that fly*
> *Like chaff from a threshing-floor.*
>
> Longfellow

Belle Robertson MBE looks back with gratitude on an enchanted childhood on the Mull of Kintyre, suspecting that it had more than a little to do with the fact that she stayed the course, as a competitor, well into her fifties. 'It was,' she recalls, 'all very different to the kind of scene experienced by the youngsters of today. They play, competitively, almost every week through the summer and are under constant pressure to be seen doing great things.'

Born into a farming family, Belle had an early life which centred around farm, school and church. She would have to arrive at school and church at a set hour but, in between, there was always time to linger or, as Walter Hagen would have put it, 'to stop and smell the flowers along the way'.

Take her journey home from primary school. . . . She and her companions would succumb to the aroma wafting over the wall of the smithy – and from there be drawn across the road by the smells from the meal mill. Having savoured them all, the youngsters would then 'play this exhilarating little game of jumping to and fro across the stream that drove the mill's wheels'.

'Sometimes,' she added, 'the horses would join us and paddle in the water once they had been newly shod, perhaps because the cold water acted as some kind of finishing touch.'

Not until later did Belle appreciate that that daily walk, made as it was in winter and summer and without a second thought, could well have contributed to the fact that she was to become one of the best 'bad weather golfers' the British women's game has ever known.

Nor, for that matter, did she realise that the early morning milking was paving the way for a strength which saw her out-hitting her contemporaries with room to spare.

'My job at milking,' she recalls, 'was to empty the milk into a pitcher which held about three to four gallons and then carry this pitcher

Belle Robertson winning her seventh Scottish title. St Andrews, 1986

the thirty or forty paces into the dairy. Having reached the dairy, I would then have to climb a small step and swing this heavy pitcher, first with my left hand and then with my right, so that the contents poured into a container at the top of the refrigerator.

'What I was doing, more or less, was the equivalent of what most people do today when they go to a gymnasium, the only difference being that I was reaching this high level of fitness without thinking.'

Taught by Hector Thomson at Machrihanish, Belle made her first

Miss Janice Moodie, Under-18s winner of the Ladies' British Open Amateur Stroke Play Championship, Strathaven, 1990

foray into the world of competitive golf when she went to the British Girls' championship which was to be won by Bridget Jackson at West Kilbride in 1954. Belle won the Scratch Cup at the Girls' Golfing Society meeting on the eve of the championship and was nominated for the following day's match between Scotland and England.

A member of the full Scottish side in 1958, she in 1959 reached the final of the British Women's Match-Play championship, an event she was to win in 1981.

In addition to the British Match-Play, she won the British Stroke-

Home Internationals: the winning Scotland side at Hunstanton, 1990. From left to right: Donna Jackson, Myra McKinlay, Catriona Lambert, Janice Moodie, Lesley Hope, Alison Rose, Fiona Anderson, Elaine Farquharson and Morag Wright

Play championship in 1971, 1972 and again in 1985. It was the 1985 instalment, along with the seventh Scottish title she won in 1986, at St Andrews, which led to her teeing up in the 1986 Curtis Cup match at Prairie Dunes at a time when she was fifty years of age.

In her book, *The Woman Golfer*, Belle compares the golf she played at fifty with that of her earlier golfing years:

> People often ask if I was a better player at fifty than I was in my late twenties and early thirties. There was a spell in the Sixties and early Seventies when I was probably picking up more titles than at any other stage, but I think I can safely say that I was a more complete golfer on reaching my half century.
>
> I had lost a little length but, over the years, I had shrugged off all the shyness that can be so inhibiting. At the same time, I had accumulated a wealth of experience which helped me to keep my bad rounds within the bounds of respectability. In other words, what might have been an 83 or an 84 in those earlier days would probably have been nothing worse than a 76 towards the end of my career.

Perhaps the most fascinating aspect of Belle's last years in competitive golf was that, unlike so many other great players, her putting was better than it had been at any other stage. Her explanation was simple.

Namely, that having been an indifferent putter early on, she never knew the strain of having to live up to a reputation in that department.

The improvement in her putting came as she made a study of Tom Watson's methods. From them she judged that she needed more left-hand control in her stroke, together with a shorter and firmer swing. She also followed Watson's advice in determining which was her master eye – her left, as it turned out – and thereafter resolved to keep it firmly on the ball as opposed to half following the path of her putter-head on the way back.

Belle's performance in the 1986 Curtis Cup provided a fitting climax to a career in which she featured in British teams in each decade from the Fifties to the Eighties. In what was the first occasion that any British side – Ryder, Walker or Curtis – was to win on American soil, Belle won one foursome and halved the other, with her partner Ireland's Mary McKenna.

Over lunch on the second day, Diane Bailey, the captain, had joined Belle to discuss the line-up for the last series of singles. Belle, at that time, was still in a state of grace at having holed a twelve-footer on the last green for the half point which ensured that Great Britain and Ireland could not lose the match.

She would have been happy enough to set forth in the afternoon, but both she and Diane sensed that the moment was right to give the younger players their turn.

'Shall we let you go out on a high note?' asked Diane.

Belle has done nothing to dull that glorious finish. Rather she has changed key, liking nothing so much as to study the new generation of Scottish golfers. It is a generation which, as she is the first to point out, looks better, technically, than any of the past.

Scottish players currently leading the way are Catriona Lambert, Elaine Farquharson, Janice Moodie and Mhairi McKay.

Catriona Lambert and Elaine Farquharson are interesting examples of players who, despite the lure of the women's professional circuit, have deemed it essential to have a qualification in life other than a low handicap. The former will by now be signing off at Stirling University, where she was one of the first women to benefit from a sports scholarship, while the latter, though still in her early twenties, is a fully qualified lawyer.

Janice Moodie who, at the time of writing, was an assistant in a Glasgow sports shop, is blessed with the kind of even temperament and well-planned game which should serve her well on the professional scene. As for Mhairi McKay, she is a gloriously long hitter who caught the eye of no less a personage than Tony Jacklin during the *Daily Telegraph*'s Young Golfer of the Year championships in 1991. However, with Mhairi's school teachers only marginally less enthusiastic about her work than was Jacklin about her golf, one would imagine that this level-headed soul will be taking aim on a university education.

CHAPTER FIVE

A Quartette of Double-winners

In the first hundred years of the LGU, Dorothy Campbell Hurd, Gladys Temple Dobell, née Ravenscroft, Pam Barton and Laura Davies all succeeded in winning the British championship and its American equivalent. In the case of the first three, the titles in question were amateur. Where Laura Davies is concerned, the combination was one of British and American Opens. The Ladies' British Open Championship, to give the event its official title, was started by the LGU in 1976 and belongs to that body in precisely the same way that the Open belongs to the R&A. The championship, which has attracted such illustrious overseas visitors as

Dorothy Campbell

Ayako Okamoto, Jane Geddes, Betsy King and Jan Stephenson, has been sponsored by Weetabix since 1987, and in 1992 has a purse of £300,000.

DOROTHY CAMPBELL HURD

Dorothy Bona Campbell Hurd was born in Edinburgh in 1883 and played much of her early golf at North Berwick at a time when an hour's lesson would cost 3s 6d and a day's play on the links was but a shilling.

In among her eleven major championships, Miss Campbell won the US and British Opens of 1909. It was a feat which had not been achieved before – and one which remained unmatched until Pam Barton's double of 1936.

As is so often the way, her career took off when a championship – in this case the 1905 Scottish – was held on her doorstep. Her skill and intricate knowledge of the links at North Berwick were such that she made off with the championship cup which was presented to her at the end of the week by Sheriff Melville. The performance led to her inclusion in the impromptu, seven-strong match held that year against the Americans at Cromer which the British won to the tune of 6 to 1.

The Scot, who by all accounts excelled with her little run-up shots, not only retained her title at Cruden Bay in 1906, but won for a third time in 1908 when her victim in the final was the unfortunate Miss Cairns. The latter was three down after five holes and lost the sixth when her caddie accidentally kicked her ball.

When Miss Campbell defeated Florence Hezlet in the 1909 British championship at Birkdale, the final moved one George Harold to verse. . . .

Two fair ladies bravely striving,
Each with mighty heart:
Now they're putting! Now they're driving!
With consummate art.

Two fair ladies, dainty graceful –
Nervous? not at all;
Of the thronging crowd unmindful;
Philosophical;
Though a fate, unkind and cruel,
Hang o'er all they do,
Yet how well they take their 'gruel'
'Sportsmen' through and through.

Miss Campbell took up an invitation to play in the American championship of that year at Merion. She duly won and, so taken was she with that continent as a whole, she stayed on, returning to these shores only as a visitor.

In 1910 she won the US Amateur and the Canadian Amateur, while in 1911 she picked up her second British title. Her homecoming, from what we can gather, caused quite a stir.

Eleanor E. Helme, in her book *After the Ball*, explained that though, after the defeat of Cecil Leitch and Gladys Ravenscroft, the championship was wide open, 'No one really suspected that Miss Campbell would come through. . . . A Canadian winter was hardly the perfect preparation for winning a championship: even a Scot has not yet played golf on snowshoes and the deck of an Atlantic liner provides an expensive and not wholly satisfactory teeing ground. Perhaps she was a little lucky in the draw, but it is not everybody who can turn luck to such good account as did Miss Campbell. She played herself steadily into form, getting a little better with each succeeding round. . . .'

Six years after she won the 1924 US Amateur, at the age of forty-one, Mrs Campbell Hurd was still playing well enough to give a game to the best. Indeed, in writing for a British audience on the Americans they would be seeing at Sunningdale in that precursor of the Curtis Cup in 1930, this normally modest soul let slip the fact that, in an exhibition game the week before, she had defeated the young Glenna Collett.

GLADYS TEMPLE DOBELL (née Gladys Ravenscroft)

Miss Ravenscroft, who was born in Rock Ferry, Cheshire, in 1888, was a good all-round sportswoman who was representing her county at hockey until Fred Robson, of Ryder Cup fame, advised that she should stop.

It could be that Robson felt it would be easier to impose a more conventional style on his young pupil were the hockey to be forgotten, but her golf remained the reverse of orthodox, although it was never ungainly. She would hold the club with her right hand 'right underneath the grip with the fingers heavenwards for the long shots', while her putting method was still more curious. She would face the hole and putt with the ball outside the right foot.

Though Dorothy Campbell had won the British of 1911 at Portrush, the match of the championship was, by all accounts, the Tuesday morning game involving Gladys Ravenscroft and Cecil Leitch. Miss Ravenscroft, though she had not slept a wink on the Monday night, ultimately won at the twenty-second after Miss Leitch had topped her ball.

But that win, coupled with the ensuing excitement – 'everybody cheered themselves hoarse for both of them' – left Miss Ravenscroft with nothing left to give in her afternoon game against Miss Bourn and she lost on the last green. Miss Bourn, we are told, was nearly in tears at finding herself responsible for so dastardly a deed.

Twelve months later and Miss Ravenscroft met Miss Leitch again. This time it was in the semi-final, with the venue Turnberry. Once more, the match was a close one . . . . Though Miss Ravenscroft was three up with four to play, Miss Leitch, 'knowing she was now in a tight corner, played with wonderful pluck and infused much drama into the closing stages of the match'.

Gladys Temple Dobell, née Ravenscroft

The Silloth golfer won each of the fifteenth and sixteenth and halved the seventeenth to be just one to the bad mounting the last tee. Great competitor though she was to become, Miss Leitch, at that point, was still considered to be a little suspect in terms of temperament.

Having played herself back into contention against Miss Ravenscroft, she promptly shanked her approach. Miss Ravenscroft was through to the final, where she defeated Miss S. Temple by 3 and 2.

In those days, when there was not the diversity of sports that there is today, the fame attached to being the leading British woman golfer of the day would stretch far beyond the golfing firmament. *Hearth and Home*, the *Ideal Home* of the day, opened their article on the new champion with the following question:

'How does it feel to be the champion, to be the First Lady in the World of Golf, to be at the very top of the tree?'

'That has never occurred to me,' replied Miss Ravenscroft, quietly. 'One just obeys one's natural instinct to do one's best; it is not a matter of fighting or beating, it is that nothing less than the very best is satisfying to the demands of one's disposition.'

'Then it isn't a spirit of rivalry that possesses you. . . .'

Miss Ravenscroft paused before replying: 'There is just that about golf that prevents all pettiness, jealousy, rivalry and the like. The wind playing about one, the far-stretching turf and one's healthful action are antidotes against such littleness of mind.'

When pressed on the subject of golf and romance, Miss Ravenscroft replied, 'The golf girl does not regard every man as a possible lover; she has her own interests. Her life and her mind are pleasantly occupied, she is capable, self-reliant, happy and content.'

This was not the defensive talk of one who had no romance in her life, for Miss Ravenscroft had been engaged to Mr Temple Dobell since 1909. What is more, she was an uncommonly good-looking girl – tall, lissom, with 'a head covered with the most engaging of sausage curls'.

Though Miss Ravenscroft failed to defend her British title in 1913, she entered the American Amateur championship of that year. As luck would have it, she drew her close friend Muriel Dodd, the new British champion, in the semi-final. It was billed as the most inviting of prospects, but Miss Ravenscroft never lost a hole. 'Gladys,' said an American golf-writer, 'outdrove Miss Dodd by many yards from nearly every tee and supplemented 200-yard drives with fine approaches.'

In the final, the Cheshire golfer defeated Mary Hollins by two holes, Miss Hollins having played her match of matches against Harriot Curtis in the other semi-final.

Not long after her marriage, Mrs Dobell, who won no fewer than twelve Cheshire championships, lost by a yawning 10 and 8 margin to

Miss Leitch in what was the second instalment of the English championship. 'Miss Leitch,' ran a newspaper article, 'has improved her game beyond all recognition; Mrs Dobell has practically stood still.'

If her confidence was a little dented, her love of the game was unscathed. Indeed, this game competitor was a runner-up in the Cheshire championship at the age of sixty and again at sixty-one – and was still the owner of a six handicap when she died at seventy-one.

The late Bah Nottingham, Mrs Temple Dobell's daughter, was speaking during a visit to the 1989 British Seniors' championship at Wrexham, of how her mother had had one piece of advice which she never failed to pass on to youngsters anxious to give themselves every possible chance. 'A good caddie,' she would say, 'is always worth a shot or two.'

Obviously, things might have been different had she played today, but Mrs Temple Dobell was inclined to go along with that old saw about a bad workman blaming his tools. She never changed her clubs – and her daughter, in turn, felt much the same way about making sparing use of equipment.

Indeed, Mrs Nottingham, at her best a nine handicap golfer, used just six clubs before deciding that the time had come to think again. At which point she discarded a couple more, leaving herself with a four wood, five iron, seven iron and putter.

PAM BARTON

The story goes that Pam Barton, who held the British and US titles of 1936, was a golfer whose cheerful exterior – she had short red hair, a freckled face and a ready smile – masked a total dedication to the game.

Her sister, Mervyn Sutherland Pilch, who, at seventy, was still scoring in the seventies and is no mean player today, is quick to refute that picture.

'She was never that single-minded', explained Mrs Sutherland-Pilch, before going on to talk of the social engagements which would punctuate Pam's golf schedule; and of the way in which, on a golfing trip abroad, she would savour a great deal more than merely the golf.

It was at a time when Pam was twelve, and Mervyn two years older, that the sisters went for their earliest lessons from the great J. H. Taylor at Royal Mid-Surrey. . . .

'He hadn't a clue how to teach,' said Mrs Sutherland Pilch, irreverently, of the five-times Open champion. 'He would stand there with his big stick and say "You've got to hit it." But with our little wrists we couldn't begin to hit the kind of shots he had in mind.'

An octogenarian uncle, whom they met for a first time after a day's foursomes at Ranelegh, home of the early international matches, paid for the girls to go to Archie Compston at Coombe Hill.

Mrs Sutherland Pilch, who also went on to play for England, remembered Compston as being a great teacher, albeit one who was more than a little brutal: 'He had us hitting balls until we were flat on our faces.' Nor did he manage much in the way of encouragement, with his most oft-repeated exhortation, 'You're a lousy couple of girls. . . . I'll never make anything out of you.'

Where Mervyn will tell you that she herself was bone idle, Pam, who loved hitting balls on the practice ground, worked with relish on Compston's recommendation that she should shorten her swing and go through the ball with firm hands and forearms. In all, she shortened her action by what felt, to her, like a foot, but what was probably no more than two or three inches.

Though there were always comments to the effect that Mervyn, who was much the taller, had the more graceful-looking swing, it was Pam who had the greater will to win.

When, for example, she defeated Mervyn in the course of what was the last British Girls' championship for which Mervyn was eligible, word has it that she was genuinely sorry – but only after she had holed the winning putt.

Pam's lone pilgrimage, as a nineteen-year-old, to the 1936 US Open at Canoe Brook, was in itself a courageous act. When she won, Bernard Darwin described it as an achievement, 'which can perhaps only be appreciated by those who have experienced the difficulties of playing as a stranger, however hospitably received, in a strange land.'

Darwin's abiding memory of her matching win in the British championships was one of watching her straighten out the path of her putting backswing: 'She went to a vacant green, laid down two clubs so that the shafts made a groove for the head of her putter and practised away relentlessly up and down the straight line.'

Just how unaffected she was by this double success is best summed up by a recollection from Jean Bisgood, English champion in 1951, 1953 and 1957.

'It was at a time when she held both titles that my father and I bumped into Pam at Royal Mid Surrey. My father asked if she would take a quick look at me on the practice ground. She could easily have made excuses, but she must have spent a good hour watching me hit balls.'

Enid Wilson's memories of the young Miss Barton tally with those of Miss Bisgood. 'It is terribly difficult,' wrote Miss Wilson, 'for a young golfer always to do and say the right thing. If she remains silent in deference to her elders, she is accounted dumb; if she makes bright conversation and tries to entertain her companions, she is precocious. Miss

Barton had the happy knack of being able to say and do the right things in whatever company she found herself, and she was most popular with the old people and a favourite with the young. She was a splendid sportswoman, modest, unassuming and thoughtful of others.'

Nor was her modesty affected by the second British title she won in 1939 at Portrush. As skilfully and disarmingly as ever, she would dodge any in-depth conversation concerning what made her a champion. However, there came an evening, when golfing battles had long since been superseded by war and she was in the WRAF, that she was happy enough to unleash her innermost golfing thoughts.

The occasion was a chance meeting at Manston with Laddie Lucas, a former journalist and Walker Cup player who was at the time commanding the Spitfire Wing at Coltishall in Norfolk. As they relaxed over dinner, Lucas – there are few more avid students of the game than he – listened intently as his companion told him that she had started off in golf with the feeling that she ought to be able to win. 'Why, I don't know; but the feeling was there, rather like one gets a premonition that something is going to happen.'

As Lucas relates in his book, *The Sport of Prince's*, Pam went on to divulge how, long before she had learnt to play properly, she felt she played better 'when I was excited and things mattered'.

Less than a fortnight after that conversation, Pam Barton, then twenty-six, was dead. The manner of her death, as recalled by Henry Cotton, with whom she had often played at Ashridge, reflected the *joie de vivre* which had lit her golfing exploits.

'After a dance at a nearby Officers' Mess, her pilot boyfriend, who had borrowed a little training plane from their home air-field, decided, in order not to fly over the Officers' Mess and risk an enquiry into what a plane was doing in the air at that time of the early morning, to push the plane on to the grass and take off downwind.'

Its tail caught a building at the end of the field. Both were killed outright.

LAURA DAVIES

In 1984, the LGU selectors were roundly criticised when they selected a Great Britain and Ireland team for the Curtis Cup which took in not a single Scot – even though the match was at Muirfield. They could, as it turned out, just as easily have been praised for their foresight in selecting the then somewhat raw Laura Davies.

Laura knew that there were others with better credentials but, on hearing that she had been lucky enough to be named, decided to make the most of her good fortune. She was given just the two games. On the opening morning, she and Mary McKenna lost in the foursomes but, on the second afternoon, the Surrey golfer had a win she will never forget: namely, when she holed a long putt at the last to defeat the vastly more experienced Anne Sander. Later, Anne would make no secret of the fact that it was the way in which Laura had caught the last green – with an eight iron to her three-wood – which led to a second-coming in which, replete with a new swing designed to produce more length, she was chosen to play for America in the 1990 Curtis Cup.

Though Laura is too modest to want to be bracketed with so legendary a figure as Lady Heathcoat-Amory, it has to be said that the early years of these two Surrey golfers had much in common. Both learned by imitation, with Joyce Wethered, as she was then, seizing her chances to watch such as J. H. Taylor and Harry Vardon who, between them, won eleven Open championships. Laura, for her part, was inspired by the performances of Bernhard Langer and Seve Ballesteros. She would watch them on television and when the opportunity presented itself study them in action on the practice ground. It is something she still does today, seeing such an outing almost as a refresher course.

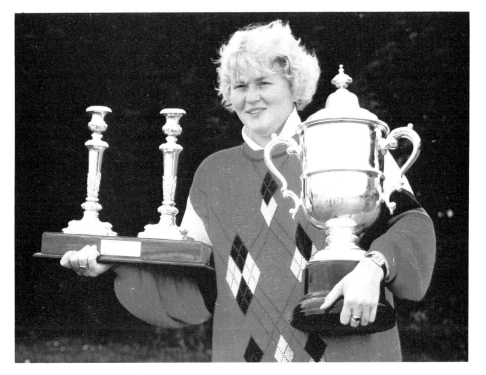

Laura Davies. A historic moment in which, on her arrival at St Mellion for the 1987 Weetabix British Open, she holds aloft the British Open Trophy she won at Birkdale in 1986 and the American Open Trophy. She had just returned from America where she had beaten JoAnne Carner and Ayako Okamoto in an 18-hole play-off. Though she had no time to practise before St Mellion, Laura finished second behind Alison Nicholas

'When I look at them,' she explained in her recent autobiography, 'I am trying, first and foremost, to pick up their rhythm. Having watched them hit a few shots, I play those shots over and over in my head, almost as I would a song. Then, when I go to the practice ground, all I am trying to do is to reproduce that timing and feel.'

Both Miss Wethered and Laura played much of their early golf with men. Miss Wethered would go out alongside her brother, Roger, while Laura would set off with her brother, Tony, and his friends. Miss Wethered spelt out the advantages in her books, *Golfing Memories and Methods*:

'Playing with men stronger and better than oneself is the quickest and the most certain way of improvement for a girl. It meant that when I played in ladies' matches, the difference from being continually outdriven and outplayed made the game seem much easier and gave one additional confidence.'

Both women were ushered into the Surrey team more on promise than performance. In the case of Miss Wethered, it was one Lady Rigby who, noting how Joyce could hold her own with Roger and his acquaintances, suggested she be given a place in the county side of 1920. Along much the same lines, Laura was picked out in 1982 by Joan Rothschild, a far-sighted official who went on to become president of Surrey and later of England.

Mrs Rothschild had been among those watching the 1982 Surrey Junior championship in which Laura, after arriving at the turn in a 48 inflated by such disasters as a six-putt green, had come home in 36. That left her level with Sally Prosser, who today plays alongside her on the professional tour.

The two set off down Sunningdale's first hole, a par five of 450 yards, and Laura caught the green with a drive and eight iron en route to an unanswerable eagle.

Belle Robertson, who won the Scottish championship a record seven times, was another who, like Joan Rothschild, spotted that Laura had rather more to offer than length. In *The Woman Golfer*, Belle comments:

It only seems like yesterday that I had my first sight of Laura. She was playing against Mary McKenna in the British Women's championship at Walton Heath. I had been told what to expect in terms of the length she hit the ball but I had also been led to believe that that was all she could do; that her short-game was virtually non-existent. It was at the fifteenth hole that I suddenly saw for myself that she had got the lot. She had hit her ball into sand and could scarcely have been faced with a more difficult shot in that there was only a yard or so of green between the bunker's edge and the flag. Even before she hit the ball, there was something about the way she settled to it that told me she knew exactly what she was about. Her shot was a beauty, one which smacked of touch and talent. The other thing which struck me about Laura that day was her lovely attitude; she exuded the same compelling calmness and control that I had seen before in Marley Harris.

Many had hoped that Laura would stay in the amateur game after the Curtis Cup of 1984. Yet, much though she enjoyed the team side of things and the friendly golf she would play at West Byfleet, Laura felt at the start of 1985 that the time had come when she should be earning her own living. Her old headmaster had once indicated that that was something she would never do on a golf course.

Armed with a £1,000 loan from her mother which she was able to pay back in the first fortnight, she won the 1985 Belgian Open and finished her first season atop the money-list. What is more, her confidence was given a further boost by the tribute she received from Betsy King, the American who played with her in the British at Moor Park. 'If Laura were ever to fulfil her potential,' said Miss King, the winner that week, 'she would leave me for dead.'

Betsy was in the field the following year when Laura won the Open at Royal Birkdale. It was a week when Laura, an inveterate gambler since the days when she and her grandmother would spend their Saturday afternoons watching horse racing on television, had seen Debbie Dowling, a sister Surrey player to whom she had lost money over the practice days, as the most likely winner of the £9,000 first prize.

Laura herself played 34 uninspired holes before pulling up eagle, birdie to be just five shots to the rear of America's Peggy Conley at the half-way stage.

In round three, the excitement mounted as she stood over a nine-yard putt offering the chance of an eagle and a 67. To her dismay, she spilt three putts to hand in an anti-climactic 69.

Three to the rear of Peggy Conley, she made up the difference in the first two holes of the final afternoon, opening birdie, eagle, to the American's par, par. Instead of feeling quietly satisfied at making so safe a start, Miss Conley was understandably not a little shaken.

Laura went ahead with a birdie at the short seventh and never lost the upper hand. She admitted to being a shade nervous over the closing holes, but those nerves were as nothing to the ones which surfaced when she had to make her winner's speech.

'I hate that side of things,' she confessed, before admitting, amid the euphoria, that there were times in her amateur days when she had taken aim on second place in a bid to avoid having to say anything.

The winner of a total of £37,500 on the European tour of that year,

Laura in 1987 finished second in Europe and performed the astonishing feat of winning the US Open at Plainfield after a play-off with JoAnne Carner and Ayako Okamoto.

Laura's easy-going attitude paid dividends over what was a long and difficult week. It was typical of her, for example, that on the day when play was cancelled because of a storm, she remained unmoved by the sight of all her sister competitors on the practice ground, driving past them without a second thought on her way back to the hotel. Indeed, the nearest she got to playing any golf that day was to engage in a putting contest down the hotel corridors.

There could scarcely have been a more popular winner. Everywhere one went at Plainfield there were strong men huddled together discussing which club Laura had taken where. One suspects that her name will forever be associated with their 493 yards seventeenth where she made a habit of arriving on the green in two. Amid the ensuing applause on the third day, Plainfield's oldest member maintained that no woman had ever come close to doing such a thing before – and further noted that it was so rare for a man to reach the green in two that the player in question was certain to command a paragraph in the club's newsletter.

Up until the time of writing, Laura has won on one or other side of the Atlantic, or both, every year since turning professional. There are those who maintain that she should have won more; that she is not the force she was in 1987.

One school of thought has it that she should work harder on her game; another that she should give up being her own teacher. What would strike more of a chord with Laura, maybe, is Catherine Lacoste de Prado's theory that it can take time 'to swallow' a major success.

A relatively late starter, Laura, twenty-nine in 1992, is nowhere near burnt out in terms of competitive fire. It helps, too, that she simply loves her golf. Indeed, she is on record as saying that, if the professional circuits of America and Europe were to collapse tomorrow, she would be looking for her old place in the Surrey team.

Carrying the Generation Gap
by J. H. Taylor

The weakest point of a woman's game is generally in driving. Here it is that wrist-play comes into operation, and the absence of this power in ladies militates against full and complete success. The stronger the wrist, the longer the 'carry' it is possible to get upon the ball; so with stronger wrists and forearms it is not at all a matter for surprise that men should prove themselves capable of driving a longer ball than their sisters or wives.

The absence of sufficient wrist power is also noticeable in the playing of the iron and intermediate strokes, so that a woman, in order to make the best use of the power she possesses, cannot afford to throw any chances aside and must be careful in watching that she does not unwittingly allow herself to develop any bad points, always difficult to tone down or remove successfully.

from *Taylor on Golf*, 1902

Laura Davies, 1991

I honestly feel that most women golfers have what it takes to hit the ball farther than they do. To my way of thinking, the greatest fault of the middle and higher handicap golfer is one of failing to give the ball a genuine clout.

This could have something to do with husbands constantly advising their wives to put down an old ball here and an old ball there, for I get the impression that it is less a physical than a mental problem. Whatever the reason, it is a pity, because these players I have in mind are mostly beautifully taught in terms of set-up and takeaway, and the trouble stems from decelerating or collapsing on the down-swing.

The best thing they could do to get over this problem is to listen to the crash of ball on clubhead engendered by a hard-hitting man.

Joyce Wethered and Glenna Collett

CHAPTER SIX

A Linking of Legends

Nothing in the first hundred years of women's golf has been more fortunate than that Glenna Collett, the greatest amateur in America, and Joyce Wethered, her British counterpart, should coincide. It was not just in the matter of golf that the two were out on their own. The feminine charm with which each plied her skill led to the conversion of golfing misogynists the world over, while the sportsmanship of the two players was endlessly refreshing. No one had a bad word to say about either woman.

Herbert Warren Wind, America's most revered golf writer, said of Glenna, 'Young men wrote poems about her infinite charms as she stood silhouetted against the horizon at Pebble Beach; older men claimed that she was the exact type William Dean Howells had in mind when he had stated that the crowning product of America was the American girl.'

Such praise was on a par with what Walter Hagen had to say about Joyce Wethered: 'As I watched her, I thought there wasn't a male golfing star in the world who wouldn't envy the strong, firm type of stroke she played. . . . She hit her shots crisply like a man expert, but without having any mannish mannerisms to detract from her charm as a quiet and gracious young sportswoman.'

Hagen was the man who recommended that women should concentrate more on Medal-Play, his reasoning being along the lines that Match-Play tended to bring out the worst in its female exponents.

But the contests involving Glenna Collett and Joyce Wethered – and they took in a couple of the game's classics – epitomised all that is best in Match-Play. The two loved to give themselves wholeheartedly to a good scrap and each was unstinting in her praise of the other.

In recalling the circumstances of her win over Glenna in the 1929 final of the British Women's championship at St Andrews, Lady Amory said, 'It was a truly wonderful moment. I had wanted this win at St Andrews so badly and, with Glenna being such a grand opponent, that match was everything a good match ought to be.'

Of the many tributes Glenna paid to Miss Wethered, there is none more telling than that chivalrously generous, but clearly heartfelt, plaudit made in the wake of their 1925 encounter in the semi-final stages of the British at Troon: 'She is as near perfection as I ever dreamed of being when I sat in a deep-seated rocker on the front porch in the cool summer evening years ago and dreamed my best dreams.'

Glenna Collett Vare

Born 20.6.1903. Died 1989
US Amateur champion 1922, 1925, 1928, 1929, 1930, 1935
Canadian champion 1923, 1924

Runner-up British championship 1929, 1930
Curtis Cup 1932, 1936, 1938, 1948 (capt. 1934, 1936, 1948. Non-playing captain 1950)

Lady Heathcoat-Amory, *née Wethered*

Born 17.11.1901
British champion 1922, 1924, 1925, 1929
English champion 1920, 1921, 1922, 1923, 1924
Curtis Cup 1932 (playing captain)

Crowd scene from the 1929 British Championship at St Andrews. When Joyce Wethered won at the 35th, she and Glenna, to use the champion's own words, were 'torn apart and became the centre of a squeezing, swaying and almost hysterical mob, shouting and cheering themselves hoarse'

Rough-hewn in that neither spoon was played from the fairway, Joyce Wethered (left) and Glenna Collett demonstrate much of the poise and balance indelibly associated with their great contemporary, Bobby Jones

GLENNA COLLETT VARE

It was in 1984 that Glenna Collett Vare, then eighty-one, was a guest of the Ladies' Golf Union for the Curtis Cup at Muirfield. The inaugural St Rule Trophy was being held over the Old Course, St Andrews, during the previous weekend and Mrs Vare had accepted an invitation to look again at the links where, some fifty-five years before, she had lost to Joyce Wethered in that most famous British Women's final of all time.

With the course abuzz with members and competitors, this living legend declined the offer of a stroll down the first fairway. Instead, she stood at the top of the steps beside the eighteenth green, looking out over the course and back across the years.

For one reason or another, her manner was such as to put one in mind of a passage in Joyce Wethered's *Golfing Memories and Methods*. In it, Miss Wethered was examining the enviably 'detached attitude' possessed by her great rival: 'She intrudes her presence to the smallest degree upon her opponents. I would even say that she appears to withdraw herself almost entirely from everything except the game, and her shots alone remind one of the brilliant adversary one is up against. If she is finding her true form, then there is little hope, except by a miracle, of surviving – at any rate in an eighteen-hole match. But there are also some vague days in between, when her interest and concentration seem to be elsewhere.'

On being approached by a St Rule Trophy contestant with a question about her favourite memories from the 1929 final, Mrs Vare started from her reverie. 'It's too long ago to remember,' she murmured, before shrugging off the past with a counter-question as to how her young companion had fared that day.

In keeping with the way in which she played 'the greatest match of my life' at St Andrews, the American was taught by a Scot. Alex Smith of Carnoustie was the professional in question, he having been among five well-known golfers who set out from Scotland on 19 March 1898, 'to teach the Americans the Royal and Ancient game and also for the purpose of engaging in clubmaking'.

Winner of the American Open both in 1906 and 1910, Smith had been hailed as 'the longest hitter in the field, save perhaps Braid', in the 1905 Open at St Andrews. His hard hitting was something he passed on to the young Glenna Collett. She always hit the ball farther than her peers. Also, as Joe Dey, that most distinguished of American officials, noted in his column in *Golf Digest*, she apparently led the way among American women in terms of playing not just for the green but for the flag.

Like many a good teacher, Smith kept his advice simple, often reiterating the same point. In exemplification of this, Mrs Vare told Jim Dodson, in a 1989 edition of *Golf Magazine*, that Smith would ask her to hit a few balls before pronouncing, 'That's enough. Remember to get your heel down quickly.' Mrs Vare added that she had over the years become more and more aware of how this was a movement which almost all the good golfers, not excluding Jack Nicklaus, had in common: 'Where Smith was concerned, if I remembered to do that, I was pretty good.'

Initiated to golf by her father, who won the French Cycling championships on the day she was born, Mrs Vare said of her first eighteen holes: 'I don't remember a more unpleasant afternoon. Struggling along, missing more shots than I made, getting into all sorts of hazards, and finishing with the embarrassing score of 150.'

The inspiration which fuelled her championship career came that day in 1917 when, as a fifteen-year-old, she went to watch an exhibition match which included Bobby Jones, also aged fifteen, and Alexa Stirling, who had not long before won the first of her US Amateur titles.

Jones and Miss Stirling, who had grown up playing alongside each other at the East Lake Course, Atlanta, were in the midst of a series of such matches in aid of the Red Cross – and it was in these circumstances that Jones claimed to have learned to keep his temper under control: 'I heaved numerous clubs, and once threw the ball away. I read the pity in Alexa's soft brown eyes and finally settled down, but not before I had made a complete fool of myself.'

After watching their game, Mrs Vare, who in 1965 was to receive the Bobby Jones Award for distinguished services to golf, returned to her home course and, for a first time, took fewer than fifty for nine holes. 'I was,' she marvelled, 'like one inspired. I did not think of my stance, of my hands and feet in connection with my swing. All I did was to endeavour to hit the ball and I must say there was a decided improvement.'

In 1925, when she won the second of her six US Amateur championships, Mrs Vare defeated the same Alexa Stirling she had so admired that day. The score was a resounding 9 and 8, although it was not to be her most emphatic scoreline in the context of a US Amateur final. That was a 13 and 12 affair in the 1928 final in which the player on the receiving end was Virginia van Wie.

Aside from her record haul of US Amateur titles, Mrs Vare won the Canadian Ladies' championships of 1923 and 1924 and the French championship of 1925.

National titles apart, she won a string of the major regional events in the States – a little matter of seven Easterns and six Norths and Souths.

'Being a champion,' she once said, feelingly, 'is quite a job . . .' She thought about it a lot and came to the conclusion that it was hard, as a champion, to stay the same: 'Sooner or later the champion begins to realise that she is supposed to do this and that, either to be agreeable or through an honest wish to live up to the sweet things said about her in the sports columns. So the title-holder becomes a bit of an actress, creating a professional manner. That's the insidious thing about being a champion. You change inside, or outside. But you change, anyhow.'

What she found particularly difficult was trying to be 'a good sport' when it came to the social side of a tournament. At times, when she wanted nothing so much as to get to her bed, she would have to don a dress and put in an appearance at a cocktail party, or some such social event.

Though capable of the kind of overwhelming defeat she inflicted on Virginia van Wie, Mrs Vare refuted Dodson's suggestion that she must have been 'a fierce competitor'. Early on in her career she had often failed to put away opponents of whom she clearly had the beating. Indeed, Herb Warren Wind at one point referred, in his paper, to how her game would fold 'like an Arab's tent'. To him, the turning point came in 1921 when she defeated Cecil Leitch in the Berdthellyn Cup competition in Philadelphia. 'Almost overnight,' said Wind, 'Glenna became a different golfer, a confident golfer. She started to hit out, to strike her shots as forcefully as she did on the practice fairway.'

She herself felt there was a weak link in her competitive make-up all her days, for she found it genuinely difficult to play against the opponent who was clearly afraid of her: 'I'd start out on the first tee with a girl saying how scared she was of me. So I'd get kind of sentimental and want to put her at ease, and before I knew it I'd be five down and licked.'

Not that she would ever have put forward such an explanation at the time. . . .In Joyce Wethered's view, Glenna was 'unequalled in the generous-minded and sporting attitude that was natural to her. She has never been a player quick to protest against the misfortunes of a round. On the contrary, she has taken her defeats as well as her victories with a calm philosophy that nothing can move.'

Though she had preferred to keep her memories to herself during her last visit to St Andrews, Mrs Vare never forgot the details of the 1929 final. Just as Lady Amory not so long ago gave the author a complete picture of the match from her point of view, so Mrs Vare, just a few months before her death, was telling Dodson how she had been 'five up at the turn in the morning and missed a putt at the twelfth that would have put me six up. Then she [Wethered] won three of the next six holes coming in. In the afternoon, she was four up by the turn. Then I started to win a few back. It's funny. In the morning when I was ahead, the gallery was deathly quiet. When Wethered started to come on in the afternoon, the crowd began to pick right up and make noise. She holed what the British call a 90-yard putt and won on the seventeenth hole and that was that. But the crowd went a little mad. The Scots, nice as they are, really were pulling for her. The bobbies had to escort both of us to the clubhouse. I think if I'd beaten Joyce Wethered that day, I wouldn't be here to tell it.'

Mrs Vare's admiration for Joyce Wethered knew no bounds. 'Joyce Wethered,' she wrote in her delightful book, *Ladies in the Rough*, 'is all that you would expect a real English girl to be. Affable and pleasant, courteous, reserved, gentle-mannered. And golf! Well, she is as good as it is possible to be. . . .As a stylist, she is as fine as Bobby Jones. She has the unruffled calm of Walter Hagen, the confidence of Gene Sarazen, and the fighting spirit of Jesse Sweetser.'

The American returned to play in the British in 1930, when it was at Formby, and was definitely the favourite when she came up against the relatively unsung Diana Fishwick in the final. In the account of the match in *Fairway and Hazard*, the reporter, in looking back to the moment when the two appeared on the first tee, said that it was 'almost pathetic to feel that all Britain's hopes were settled on one slim little figure dressed in Navy blue, who looked almost childlike. . . .'

No one gave Miss Fishwick a chance, but the teenage English underdog, who was to call her daughter after her great-hearted opponent, had her eye in on the greens and was five up at lunch. 'She can't last! She'll tire! She'll crack!' were the typically British whispers going the rounds in the clubhouse.

'There was not a sign of it when she started out again,' recorded *Fairway and Hazard*. 'In fact, she had increased her lead to six up at the sixth hole, but reached the turn with her original lead of five, both players being out in 38, excellent golf for the last half of the final.'

When the match ended in Miss Fishwick's favour at the fifteenth, 'Nothing could be heard for at least ten minutes save shouting, the crowd cheering winner, loser, referee, in fact everybody they could think of, just to let off steam and give vent to the feelings which they had been obliged to bottle up on the way round.'

Even at the tender age of twenty-five, it would seem that the American was beginning to be haunted by a premonition to the effect that the British was one title she might never win. 'More than once,' she wrote after the 1929 final, 'have I visualised myself, grey-haired and stooped, wearily trudging over the wind-swept fairways of an English course seeking that elusive title.'

It was Miss Wethered's opinion that so good a golfer as Mrs Vare was desperately unlucky not to have a record in Britain more in keeping with the one she had put together in the States. 'There is no doubt,' she wrote, 'that fortune has not treated her too kindly in her visits to this country. . . .'

Mrs Vare, who invited Miss Wethered to stay when she was in America for her exhibition tour of 1935, did not let this discrepancy in an otherwise outstanding career become an obsession. Rather did she revel in a golfing future in which she won her last US Amateur championship in 1935 and made her fourth appearance for America in the Curtis Cup in 1948 at the age of forty-five. She was either a playing or a non-playing captain of the side on no fewer than four occasions.

Along much the same lines, she moved effortlessly into the realms of officialdom, serving actively on USGA committees for fifty years. First it was on the Museum Committee, then the Women's Committee and finally the Girls' Junior Championship Committee.

At a local level, she played in the Point Judith Club championship for sixty-two years in a row. And when she reckoned that the time had come to stop playing, she derived the utmost enjoyment from watching golf on television. That is, everything except the women's game.

In an observation which could just as easily apply to much of the coverage of the distaff side of the game in these islands, she felt there was a lack of expertise in the presentation of women's golf: 'The commentators seldom properly explain what is going on. They say she's using a six iron, perhaps, but they don't tell you she's 170 yards away. Most people would be surprised that a woman can hit a six-iron 170 yards.'

Glenna Collett Vare, who died in 1989, is survived by a daughter, Glenna Vare Kalen, and a son, Edwin H. Vare III, herself knew no other way than to hit hard. She hit hard, worked hard and, at the same time, had a sense of humour which convinced everyone that she was never in any danger of taking herself too seriously.

Glenna Collett and Joyce Wethered at St Andrews on the occasion of their final in the
1929 British Women's Championship

In this vein there is a delightful tale from Enid Wilson of a practice day at Hunstanton when Mrs Vare's colleagues substituted her ball for one made by a firm whose mischievous boast it was that their missile would hook violently on those rare occasions it got off the ground.

This most sporting of competitors had not a clue as to why her game had deserted her so suddenly but, typically, fought on uncomplainingly. When all was revealed, the party's peals of laughter could be heard ringing out across the links. As you will have guessed, no one was enjoying herself more than the victim.

'Our balance should feel so comfortable and steady on the left foot at the finish of the swing that we could, if we wished, lift our right foot off the ground and still be standing on one leg with absolute security.' Joyce Wethered, Golfing Memories and Methods

CHAPTER SEVEN

Joyce Heathcoat-Amory

It was a Saturday morning and the then nine-year-old Stewart Lawson came tearing down the steps of St Salvator's, the St Andrews preparatory school which is today the Scores Hotel. Unwittingly, the headmaster had dispatched Lawson to watch a piece of history which would stay with him for rather longer than anything he had learnt in the classroom.

Lawson, for whom golf and life have always, so to speak, interlocked, was there for the start of Joyce Wethered's final in the 1929 British Women's championship over the Old Course.

The player's excitement was not so very far removed from the schoolboy's. Indeed, it had been the prospect of playing at St Andrews which had brought Miss Wethered out of the retirement on which she had embarked four years earlier: 'The magic everyone talks about at St Andrews really does exist. . . . I have always loved the way you meet the same people on the streets as on the fairways, the way in which town and course are one.'

Lawson, who down the years has held almost every R&A office there is, describes the day of the final as a little sombre – misty and grey. And he can recall being engulfed by vast numbers of spectators, all of whom were 'enthusiastic for Joyce but, as always, very fair'. An old man came to his aid. The gentleman in question had a limp and an umbrella – a perfect combination, as it turned out, for ensuring that the two of them would arrive in the front row of every gathering.

Though Lawson can remember how Joyce recovered from a five-hole deficit after nine holes to be just two down at lunch, the only shot he can still see, in his mind's eye, is her drive at the long second in the afternoon. She had already won back the first to be just one to the bad, and now she came up with this 'extraordinarily low tee shot which caught the hollow and ran on and on and on'. It left her with but a five iron to the green and, two putts later, she was back on level terms.

Let Lady Amory take up the story . . .

By the ninth, I actually stood four up, a difference of nine holes from the position at the same point in the morning round. One would imagine from the psychology of the game that the excitement of the match was now probably over, and that all would perhaps end quietly on a green four or five holes from home. From any likelihood of such a peaceful ending, I was rudely awakened by Glenna doing the next two holes in three apiece and winning them both. To lose two holes so abruptly altered the whole complexion of the game, and I must confess that I found the playing of the remaining holes a very trying experience.

The fifteenth proved crucial. After three indifferent shots, Miss Wethered had seemed in dire danger of having her two-hole lead cut to one. But she holed from six yards to hang fast to that advantage and ultimately won what she has since dubbed the match of her career at the penultimate hole.

Having performed the extraordinary feat of taking five successive English titles and four of the six British championships in which she played, it is hardly surprising that Miss Wethered's golfing background excited so much interest.

Many suggested that her success had most to do with her older brother, Roger. A Walker Cup golfer from 1921 to 1934, Roger Wethered was the man who, having tied with Jock Hutchinson for the Open championship of 1921, asked to be excused from the play-off on the grounds that he had arranged to play cricket. In the end he was prevailed upon to complete the championship but wound up with a play-off tally of 159 to Hutchinson's 150.

When Roger Wethered won the Amateur championship of 1923 at Deal, his sister, who had just lost to 'Doddie' Macbeth in the semi-finals of the British at Burnham, motored through the night in order to see him play his final. But, much though she admired him, she has never been fully convinced that he played the major part in shaping her career: 'He was two or three years older than I was and we were, in a sense, rather separate.'

Lady Amory can remember starting to play during family holidays at Bude, where it was 'windy and sunny by turn'. Her father at one time had a handicap of six. Her mother, on the other hand, fought a continuous if losing battle with the LGU's handicapping system: 'She had a terrible struggle trying to get her handicap cards out.'

There were further holidays in Dornoch, where the family had a house with a front window within hooking distance of the second tee, and Lady Amory can remember, vividly, how she and her brother used to keep 'temperature charts' on bedroom walls showing how their scoring had shaped from day to day. Indeed, when she was introduced to the youngest competitor in the British at Wentworth in 1980, Lady Amory advised her to do the same.

She has memories of one formal lesson but, basically, did everything by imitation. Her father often took her and Roger to see players like Harry Vardon and J. H. Taylor in action and she will tell you how, later on, she was tremendously influenced by Bobby Jones.

'After watching Bobby Jones,' said Lady Amory, 'I made my backswing longer and endeavoured to have the club pointing to the hole at the top. My swing probably never did look like his – but I liked to think that it did.'

Oddly enough, she has never, to this day, seen any kind of film of her own action but, of the many compliments paid to this great golfer, one suspects that Walter Hagen's words must have meant as much as any: 'Comparing Wethered with some other star women players, who I will not mention by name because life is very sweet to me, it seems that the strength of her game was in its strictly feminine characteristics. She had grace, timing and touch.'

Bobby Jones, for his part, thought she had the best swing of anyone – man or woman – he had ever seen. Not only that, but he owned to having had the feeling that he had been 'outclassed' by her.

Where Roger Wethered definitely contributed to his sister's golfing development was in getting the golfing friends he made during his years at Oxford. Among them was Cyril Tolley, whom she would one day beat to the tune of five and three in the course of a Surrey–Middlesex match which drew a gallery of a thousand.

For Joyce, the spring of 1920 took in many matches with Roger and his fellow undergraduates but, even if such encounters stretched her play, she had no reason to feel much confidence when she headed for Sheringham and that year's English Women's championship. After all, in the context of the Surrey county side, she had been playing as low as sixth.

A friend by name of Molly Griffiths had suggested that they make the Sheringham trip together and the Wethered parents, who had no particular ambition for their daughter at that stage, had left the decision entirely to her.

In the qualifying round, her 'very indifferent' score of 94 neither depressed her unduly nor raised expectations in anyone else. But, when it came to the Match-Play, she had a carefree run to the final, where her opponent was Cecil Leitch, the holder. 'No one,' confirmed Victoria Gillieson, a sister competitor that week who was to die in 1991, the year the English Women's championship paid a return visit to Sheringham, 'thought that Joyce Wethered could win. . . . In truth, no one had wavered from the view that Cecil would take the title.'

Joyce Heathcoat-Amory

Lady Amory has often spoken of her matches with Cecil as being altogether different from those she had with Glenna Collett in that, with Miss Leitch attracting a certain band of followers who were hell-bent on seeing their player win, there was always an uncomfortable edge to the proceedings.

'People either adored Cecil Leitch or they didn't,' she explained in an interview for a 1984 edition of *Golf Monthly*. 'She was the big noise in women's golf when I came on the scene and what made her stand out still more was the fact that she had so dominant a personality. Perhaps because I had this ability to disappear in a cocoon of concentration, I was never mesmerised by Cecil to the same extent as some of the others. In truth, I seldom watched her hit a shot. She gave the ball a marvellous thump, but her rhythm was not one to copy in that it was very hard, very fast.'

At Sheringham, in their first meeting, things went according to forecasts as Miss Leitch went into lunch with a four-hole lead – and made it six as she won the first two holes of the afternoon.

Sheringham in June was dry and playing short and, after gnawing away at that lead, Miss Wethered suddenly came up with three successive threes from the eleventh to give her vastly more experienced adversary real cause for concern. Then, following a dramatic approach to a blind hole – her ball finished but a foot from the flag – she was back to all square with three to play.

By this time she could sense, very keenly, that the winning of this game mattered very much more to her opponent than it did to her. In fact, the atmosphere was such that she was half inclined to think that things would be a lot more peaceful if Miss Leitch were to win. But the writing was on the wall and, with Miss Leitch having been shattered by the change of fortunes, Miss Wethered won on the green of the seventeenth.

There is a railway running alongside Sheringham's seventeenth and, though the tale has been solemnly attached to almost every links she ever played which had a railway line, Lady Amory has confirmed that it was here that the 'train' incident must have occurred. At the end of the final the attendant golf writers had asked the winner how much she had been disturbed by the train which rattled past as she stood to her putt. As the whole of the golfing world knows, her innocent riposte was 'What train?'

It was noted on the last afternoon that Miss Wethered was looking a shade drawn and, by evening, she was feeling sufficiently unwell for a doctor to be summoned. Whooping cough was the diagnosis and it was to keep her 'in a state of mysterious seclusion for weeks and weeks'.

In 1921, Miss Wethered and Miss Leitch met twice; in the final of the British at Turnberry and in the final of the French Open at Fontainebleau. Miss Leitch, whose iron-play was so admired by Miss Wethered, won on both occasions to edge two-one ahead of her rival and ensure that excitement was at fever-pitch when next they met – in the final of the British at Prince's the following year.

It so happened that one of Cecil Leitch's greatest fans, an Irishman by name of Mr Summerville, had been chosen to act as referee. At the end of a superb morning's golf, the match was square but when, after lunch, Miss Leitch began to falter and Miss Wethered pulled ahead, the said Mr Summerville threw his hat to the ground, began to weep and had to retire. 'That,' said Lady Amory, 'didn't help Cecil. And then there was the business of the cameras. . . .'

In those days, the cameras made a lot more noise than is the case today and, no doubt because reels of film were expensive, the photographers would start their machines running only when the player's preliminary waggle was over and he or she was taking the club back for real. Miss Leitch was upset, and seen to be upset, and duly lost at the eleventh to level the score at two matches apiece.

One point which was apparent to Miss Wethered in that particular meeting was the way in which things had turned round in terms of length. Though she had been shorter than Cecil when first they met, she was now the longer. Mind you, she was sporting enough to temper that judgment with an aside to the effect that her opponent's arm injury – it was to keep her out of golf for months – had notably reduced the strength of her iron-play.

The fifth round of the 1924 British championship at Portrush provided the next major confrontation. This was their only match over eighteen holes rather than thirty-six and, according to the *Shell Encyclopedia of Golf*, the two were like boxers sparring for an opening as they halved the first seven holes before Miss Wethered drew away to win not just that match but the championship. Lady Amory no doubt had that match in mind when she wrote of her games with Cecil: 'With us, the first sign of weakness always seemed to give an added strength to the other.'

Miss Wethered won in 1925, too, this time defeating Miss Leitch at the thirty-seventh in the British final at Troon to confirm a superiority over her rival which the public has never forgotten. That day at Troon coincided with a half-day at the dockyards and, amid the hustle and bustle of the afternoon, there was a memorable comment from a spectator who was asked to make way for the players. 'Blow the players,' said he, 'I've come to see the match.'

Though Miss Wethered had played alongside the Oxford undergraduates with no questions asked, it has to be said that the general attitude of male golfers towards their female counterparts in those years was far from enlightened. 'There were all too many clubs,' she has recalled, 'where you had the feeling you were not wanted. In fact, women mattered so little that they didn't have to pay greenfees.

'Often they wouldn't be allowed in the clubhouse and I well remember an occasion when, while waiting for my partners to emerge from the locker-rooms at Sandwich, I kept my hands and fingers warm on the radiator of someone's Rolls-Royce.'

The subject of golfing fashions in her day is one which has had Lady Amory talking, with more than a little envy, of today's vogue of slacks or a short skirt. Though the aforementioned Mrs Gillieson was recalling, just weeks before her death, how Miss Wethered's hats had furnished quite a talking-point at Sheringham, Miss Wethered has no fond memories of the golfing gear of her time.

She obviously managed to escape the conventional round felt hats of the day – 'they were awful' – but there was no alternative to the 'ghastly long skirts'. Yet, though she considered that some of the women golfers looked mannish, she says there were others who contrived to look exceedingly chic, such as Simone Lacoste and Edith Cummings.

How did the players of her generation view the powers-that-be in women's golf? 'We were rather bolshie, I'm afraid. We had to get handicap cards in and I am ashamed to say that we all considered that side of things a bit of a bore.' By all accounts, she effectively messed up the system through continuing to play off plus one at a time when others, nowhere near in the same class as herself, were down to plus two and three. In Lady Amory's defence, it had best be explained that it was because she was so busy playing with the Oxford set that she had no time for her LGU cards.

Lady Amory went on to say that she had always found the LGU ladies charming – and one can only assume that she meant it in the nicest possible way when she said of those LGU personnel she met at Wentworth in 1980, 'They haven't changed at all . . .'.

For herself, Lady Amory, unlike her old adversary, Glenna Collett Vare in the States, never got caught up in administration. 'I hated such things as committee meetings but, looking back, I feel perhaps that I should have done more.'

Her natural shyness and an inclination not to get involved, similarly contributed to a less than enthusiastic approach towards team events. She was chosen to lead Britain in the inaugural Curtis Cup match but insisted that the captain's role did not come easily. 'To be honest, I no more liked ruling others than I liked to be ruled myself. Things such as team practices appalled me. I preferred to do things in my own good time and in my own way . . .'.

Her own way, when it came to preparing for an important match, was to do everything she could to ensure that her game was as technically correct in practice as possible. Then, just before going out to play, she would cast all thoughts and theories out of her mind. 'In other words, I did everything I could before stepping out of myself and getting on with the business of playing the match. On the course, my philosophy was very much one of living the hole you were playing, of looking neither forward nor back.'

Though most choose to illustrate her uncanny powers of concentration with the aforementioned story of the passing train, Lady Amory has always been of the opinion that an incident in her 1929 final against Glenna Collett was rather more fitting.

Because of the swarming spectators on the Old Course that day, each player was allocated a steward. As luck would have it, Lady Amory's walked unnecessarily close and carried on her arm a stiff and crackling mackintosh. More and more, the lady and her mack preyed on her nerves until finally she said to herself, 'Do I say "Please move away a little" or do I make up my mind to put up with it?'

On the grounds that any kind of remonstration would lessen her concentration, she chose the latter course. Having made that decision, she forced herself to dwell no more on that walking distraction.

In her book, Lady Amory wrote:

> It is impossible to concentrate the thoughts if they are in any way vague and indefinite. That is the great difficulty in learning the golf swing. Theories abound and differ to such a degree that it is not easy to make

The 1929 England team which won the Home Internationals at St Andrews

up one's mind as to what is profitable and what is not profitable. . . .

We must first of all have our technical ideas clear in our head and then we must learn to regulate our thoughts so that our muscles will respond and perform their part of the stroke perfectly. A point of skill is reached when the good player (when in practice) plays the shots almost mechanically. This leaves the mind very much freer to concentrate on the type of shot required and to judge questions of distance and other essentials accurately.

The Twenties, in Lady Amory's opinion, represented a marvellous era in which to be involved in amateur golf. Such legendary professionals as Vardon and Braid had more or less come to the end of their reign and, though Henry Cotton was to create a resurgence of interest in the professional scene in the Thirties, there was this whole decade in which the amateur game reigned supreme. Lady Amory was insistent that this state of affairs owed as much to the writings of Bernard Darwin in *The Times* as to the players.

The Wethered family knew the Darwins well – and there were times when Joyce Wethered would stay in the Darwins' house at Aberdovey and find herself involved in some very uneasy family foursomes.

'Bernard was a shocking loser,' she said, with a twinkle. 'The bravest thing one ever did was to partner him in the mixed foursomes at Worplesdon. When you played a shot, he would stand with his black cap pulled down and his hands half over his eyes. Then, if the shot were less than perfect, there was this dreadful muttering. You could never have put up with it if you hadn't known him well and been so fond of him.'

With his problems on the greens having been largely responsible for the fact that they were taken to the twenty-second hole in their first round of the 1933 Worplesdon Foursomes, Darwin threw his putter away. Thereafter, he putted with his jigger – and they duly contrived to win.

Lady Amory loved her amateur career but there came a day when she knew she must step down. It had less to do with her family losing its fortune in the Wall Street crash of 1929 than realising that she did not want to dedicate her entire life to golf. 'Throughout the years when I was playing seriously,' she explained, 'I never lost sight of the fact that it was only a game. I had the good fortune to win when young and I was well aware of the fact that most of the fun lay in being on the attack. Once I had won the titles and it was a matter of having to defend them, the fun was not so apparent.'

She wanted time to dabble in other sports such as tennis and fishing but, more than anything, she felt in need of a change of environment. 'I met many wonderful people in golf but, maybe because of the publicity, it was difficult to make real friends. There were lots of people who would come up and make conversation but there were others – and perhaps they were the ones with whom one would have had more in common – who did not like to come up, feeling it better to stay in the background.'

Since there was, too, that element of wanting to leave home and pay her own way, she went to Fortnum and Masons and was there employed in the golf department – something which automatically rendered her a professional.

'Becoming a professional,' she maintained, 'didn't make any difference to my relationships with anybody. In fact, the four and a half years I spent there were great fun. Everybody came to me for tips and I had my own named clubs to sell. They were Hagen clubs with steel shafts but I must confess that, for myself, I preferred hickory. With hickory, one could get so much more feel with the little shots around the green.'

Lady Amory clung to her hickory clubs for very much longer than her contemporaries and she can still hear her brother saying impatiently, 'When are you going to throw them away?'

As she remembers it, Lady Amory used her hickory-shafted clubs on the four-and-a-half-month tour of America she was persuaded to make as a professional in 1935 – a tour in which she played fifty-two matches with all the top professionals and amateurs and was reputed to have earned something in the region of £4,000.

She played with Babe Zaharias and remembers this outstanding athlete for her strong forearms and her power. 'She was not particularly tall, nor was she stout. Her game was still very much in its formative stages at that point but her sheer power was very impressive.'

The Babe did not then appreciate enough about the finer points of the game to realise just how good Wethered was. 'I could hit past her drives with a two-iron,' was the Babe's less than subtle observation made in the wake of two defeats at the English player's hands.

Lady Amory played with Bobby Jones on his home course, while there was one particularly rewarding day with Gene Sarazen, a champion who will be remembered not least for the ace he scored at the Postage Stamp during the 1973 Troon Open when he was a septuagenarian. Sarazen took one look at Lady Amory's clubs and decided she needed a blaster. He gave her one of his own and that, she said, made an enormous difference to her game.

Several years later, when he was over in Scotland to make a film, Sarazen called Lady Amory when she was staying at a shooting lodge in the Cairngorms to ask if she could fit in nine holes at Blairgowrie. This she did – and the lesson she learned that day was one of the need to swing with a heavy practice club each morning in order to 'open up' her shoulders and lengthen her swing. 'That was long after I had finished playing seriously but I did heed his suggestion for a while and it did me good.'

After her spell in America, Lady Amory felt her golf was possibly better than it had been at any time in her career in that she had acquired what she called 'the professional mentality'.

Back at home, she settled quite happily into a routine which took in little more than friendly golf. She loved the weekend house-parties which were so much a part of golf at that time – and it was on one of those occasions that she met the man who was to become her husband.

The scene was Westward Ho! Dickie Gull, a member of the party, had rung his friend, John Heathcoat-Amory, at his home in Tiverton and suggested that, since he was so close, he should join them on the Saturday. 'Jack', as Sir John was always known, told how he was supposed to be playing in a match for Tiverton GC and could only come if someone was prepared to take his place.

It chanced that the captain of Tiverton had a brother staying with him who was only too delighted to fill in – all of which led to the meeting of Sir John and Joyce Wethered on the first tee at Westward Ho!

The two were engaged within three months and, on their marriage, the aforesaid Dickie Gull was able to collect five pounds as a result of a wager he had made with his friends on that first Saturday he saw the couple together.

While on the subject of wagers, Lady Amory has told, with quiet amusement, of how she was often mildly suspicious that some among her male friends had money riding on her games with them. Never, though, was she more certain that this was the case than on an occasion when she was summoned to Westward Ho! to take on 'some cricketer'. The latter had clearly been putting it about that he would have the beating of any woman golfer and it goes without saying that Sir John and his friends made it abundantly clear to Lady Amory that she had to win. Which, of course, she did.

Sir John and Lady Amory played golf together until the middle Sixties but gradually, as Sir John's arthritis became more severe, they became more immersed in building up the now world-famous garden – a garden renowned for its rhododendrons, azaleas and alpines – surrounding their Tiverton mansion, Knightshayes Court. The house, designed by William Burgess, was built by Sir John's grandfather in the late 1870s. When Sir John died in 1972, it was handed over to the National Trust, but Lady Amory still lives on in what was the former service wing on the east side of the house.

For a long time she participated fully in the running of the gardens she had done so much to create and, to this day, is ready to offer advice on new plants sent from all corners of the globe. Though some of her trophies were put on show in 1988, there were many employees at the house who, up until then, had not a clue as to her golfing past.

Though her brisk and purposeful walk at our meeting in 1984

Joyce Wethered with feline fan

suggested that a daily eighteen holes would have posed no problems for this 'Lady among Ladies', she has played no golf at all since the Sixties.

But, long though the years may be since she completed her final round, Lady Amory has always loved watching golf on television. She is inclined to dismiss her own golfing skills as 'not in the same league as the skills of a talented musician or artist', yet she has said that nothing gives her more pleasure than to settle back in her chair and watch a Jack Nicklaus or a Tom Watson in action: 'I get such a thrill from watching them on television. They are so good at what they do – and such fine ambassadors.'

It has irked her that there is so little of the women's game on television in these islands but, in 1991, she was elated at being able to tune into highlights of the Weetabix British Women's Open at Woburn. She had quesions aplenty to ask about the winner, Penny Grice-Whittaker; also, she considered the high standard of golf on that programme proof of how the women's professional game has taken root in these islands.

There has been just one occasion, in recent times, when Lady Amory stepped back into her past to see the game played 'live'. A letter arrived one morning from the sponsors of the Women's Masters tournament at Hilton Head Island, asking if she would be their guest during the championship. For a long time, she did not know what to say but, eventually, came to the conclusion that this was something she could not resist.

She was slightly concerned that she might be asked to hit a few shots during the course of the week and she laughs, still, at her brother's reaction when she picked up a club in his London home and tried a practice swing. 'Look out,' he yelled, 'you'll make a hole in the carpet.'

In the event, she never did have to play and had the most wonderful time watching the American professionals. Perhaps more than anything, she was struck by the extent to which the girls practised. 'I used to hit balls myself but it was only if something were wrong that I would hit a bucketful. As a general rule, I stopped practising the moment I started to hit the ball well. Certainly, if I had worked to the same degree as those girl professionals work before going out to play a competitive round, I would have been exhausted.'

Lady Amory could not believe that the eventual winner of that Women's Masters, Sandra Palmer, was so tiny – and she left for home convinced that the only area in which the girl professional could get still better was on the greens.

'If one had been playing now,' she reflected, 'one would have had to have been a better putter. Personally, I didn't practise putting much. I was never sure how I would putt from one day to the next and my attitude was very much one of, "I hope my putting goes well today".'

'Putting,' she added, 'has always mystified me. However much experience a man has, it does not guarantee success on the greens. Bobby Jones went through a spell when he had the jitters and was, in fact, a shocking putter towards the end of his playing days.

'In all my years,' she continued, wistfully, 'I have never quite got used to the fact that to miss by only a fraction of an inch costs the same as to miss by a foot.'

To most of those who, in the last decade, have asked to interview her about her golfing past, Lady Amory has politely excused herself on the grounds, 'It all happened so very long ago.' Yet even if she does not want to keep telling her story, that does not stop her from turning over the memories. . . .

It is not too many moons ago, for example, that she made mention of how, when she could not get to sleep at night, she would go through the holes on the Old Course, St Andrews. And of how irritated she would become when, on reaching the sixth or seventh, she would get a little confused.

'Heaven knows,' she said, feelingly, 'I ought to remember. . . . So many things happened to me out there.' With pride of place, one suspects, going to that match against Glenna Collett.

Enid Wilson by Lewine Mair

CHAPTER EIGHT

Enid Wilson

The voice which announced the final of the 1991 English Girls' championship – between Nicola Buxton of Woodsome Hall and Caroline Hall of Filton – was clipped and clear.

'Good luck, girls,' came the rider, before the two juniors smacked magnificent drives in the direction of Knole Park's first green.

It was Enid Wilson, winner of the British Girls' championship sixty-six years before, who had started the pair. Not only that, but this most spirited of onlookers, whose own golf in 1991 had received something of a setback when she injured her back lifting a sack of coal for her lounge fire, went on to follow play. While chatting away to a fellow octogenarian, the former Ryder Cup player, Sam King, Enid marvelled at the distance the modern girl could dispatch a ball.

Between times, she looked back to her own years in the game – a period which began when, as a four or five-year-old, she took her own set of miniature carpenters' tools and removed the heads from her father's hickory-shafted woods. It was a crime for which she was lucky not to be decapitated herself.

The suggestion that the juniors of the 1920s would have been rather less sophisticated than those of the 1990s met with gleefully contemptuous laughter. 'Jacqueline Gordon,' said Miss Wilson, by way of explaining herself, 'would arrive for the British Girls' dressed in silk stockings and white buckskin shoes – all from Bond Street.'

It was in 1924 that Miss Wilson's uncle suggested she should play in her first Girls' championship. The only trouble was that one had to qualify by sending in three medal cards and the said uncle had made his recommendation with just three days to go till the closing date.

Enid completed her three rounds almost on the run and, to her surprise, finished third among the sixteen who made their way through to the Match-Play stages at Stoke Poges.

Simone de la Chaume, who later married René Lacoste of Wimbledon fame, defeated Enid in the semi-finals and the elegant French player went on to beat Dorothy Pearson in the final.

The girl golfers of Miss Wilson's day, to use Miss Wilson's own words, were 'the progeny of gentlefolk'. They would mostly have picked up golf's basics from a brother or someone else in the family, but not too many would have had intensive professional tuition.

Enid, far more than the majority of her peers, appreciated the importance of a sound technique, having been taught first by her father and later by Hollinwell's Tom Williamson. She was recently the delighted recipient of a photograph of herself taken in 1931 when she was driving off Sandy Lodge's first tee in the London Foursomes. What pleased her so much was that her grip was perfect.

There were no vouchers and no postal orders to go with the trophies the young golfers would win in Enid's day. However, that the trophies in themselves were greatly prized can be gauged from her reaction to the gold medal she received for winning the Midland championship at Handsworth. She was, it is true, no more than sixteen years old at the time, but she remembers going to bed with the spoils of victory under her pillow.

She further recalls how, at that stage, she would go out to play with a pocketful of golf balls, some large, some small. A born handywoman who, in recent years, has had a lot of fun with the renovation of her oast-

Enid Wilson escaping sand

Jean McCulloch (left) meets Enid Wilson in the Scotland v England match at St Andrews, 1929

house home in East Sussex, she knew better than most which size of ball would marry best with the conditions.

It was 1931 when Enid embarked on her run of three consecutive British Women's titles – a feat which had previously been achieved only by Cecil Leitch. Enid's three finals were all comfortable affairs. She defeated both Wanda Morgan and Clementine Montgomery by 7 and 6 and, in 1933, she won by 5 and 4 against Diana Plumpton at Gleneagles.

Her Curtis Cup appearance came in May, 1932, at Wentworth, and she is apt to describe the occasion as something of a shambles. That day's lunch, it seems, is something she will never forget. . . .

The Americans, who had walked off with the morning foursomes and were to win the match 5–3, had returned to eat at Great Fosters Hotel but there was nothing laid on for the host team.

Wentworth's dining-room, where a 1932-style lunch would cost three shillings, was full to capacity. All of which led to Enid taking it upon herself to scour round the tables for left-over rolls and bits of cheese in order to feed the Great Britain and Ireland players. As this down-to-earth soul remembers it, perhaps a little uncharitably, the blame lay with the LGU: 'They consisted of a stream of Lady So-and-Sos who were not prepared to put their hands in their pockets.'

Frugal though it was, that makeshift meal yet sufficed to see Enid through a tough afternoon singles against Helen Hicks. Joyce Wethered, who had defeated Glenna Collett Vare in the match in front, had dropped back to watch her finish . . .

'The golf,' recalled Lady Amory, 'was excellent on both sides, each player taking infinite pains to leave nothing to chance. Even when the torrent of rain increased and made the conditions still more wretched, the same dour thoroughness continued right up to the seventeenth hole, where the match ended. Here Enid struck a splendid three-yard putt firmly and decisively into the hole to win by two and one.'

Twice a semi-finalist in the US Amateur championship, Enid played three times in the Home Internationals, with her only singles defeat being inflicted by Jean McCulloch in the 1929 match at St Andrews. 'All the town,' recalled Enid, 'were out watching Joyce Wethered playing the late Charlotte Beddows in the match in front and Jean and I were entirely on our own until that contest ended. Then the crowd caught up with us as we played the sixteenth and seventeenth. They came right up on to the seventeenth green and barely left us room to swing our putters. It was the only time I have ever felt scared on a golf course and the rumpus contributed to my loss.'

Never one to mince words, Miss Wilson, when interviewed recently, was dead against the women's professional tour – and that though she was made a professional herself after having written a series of captions for a swing sequence.

Having been forced into making the switch – it happened after her 1933 British win – Enid made the most of her new status, taking a job at Lillywhites and designing a complete range of golf equipment. She also built on those instructional captions, embarking on her own column in *Golf Illustrated* and becoming the *Daily Telegraph*'s women's golf correspondent.

Even though her own achievement in winning three successive British titles was never aired to the extent that would have been the case had someone else held the pen, Enid's appointment with the *Telegraph* was outstanding from the point of view of the women's game as a whole.

Her audience was kept entertained and informed, and her words served as a useful barometer to the players, most of whom had not a clue as to how they stood in the eyes of the selectors – unless, that is, they were actually named for teams. These players wanted a lead and she gave them just that. When, for instance, she noted in her column how one competitor, in her first round of the British Girls' championship of 1962, had had 'too many practice swings and preliminaries', the youngster in question, in her anxiety to please, duly set off at a gallop for her second round.

Enid, an LGU vice-president, retired from the *Telegraph* in the early

Seventies with a view to getting back to grips with her own game and to having more time for philately, an occupation with which she has busied herself since she was eight: 'I can start on it after breakfast and still be at work in the small hours of the morning,' was one not wholly surprising aside from the old champion at a time when she was well into her eighty-second year.

As was said in the *Dunlop Lady Golfer's Companion*, which was brought out a decade after her retirement, it behoves one, for the sake of future historians, to attach as many dates as possible to Miss Wilson's activities, for she would be otherwise difficult to pin down to any definite era. For example, she has never been anything other than a less-than-dedicated follower of fashion, preferring to wear a timeless tweed skirt, topped, should the need arise, by a lengthy waterproof coat.

In other areas, she has been disconcertingly ahead of the clock. When she was well into her seventies and others, many years her junior, were still a little nervous of microwave ovens, Enid was rejoicing in this latest piece of technology, installing one alongside her two Bosch cookers. 'I work on the principle that if a few people drop in they can be fed,' she said. Again, where her writing was concerned, she was similarly far-sighted. She sensed, for example, precisely how important was the first of the LGU's training schemes. Under the heading, 'The LGU's Big Experiment' she wrote:

> The big experiment by the Ladies' Golf Union in sending ten of the best juniors to be coached by John Jacobs, the professional at Sandy Lodge, is so recent that the results cannot be fully assessed, but the early sessions proved to be worthwhile on at least two counts.
>
> It is difficult to convince the young that their methods are not all that they should be when they have already achieved a certain amount of success. Girls differ very much from boys in their attitude towards the game. Boys are much more curious to know how things work and will find out for themselves how certain results are obtained.
>
> When the first ten girls went to John Jacobs, they were blissfully unaware of how and why variations in their swings produced different types of shots. After their preliminary session, they could tell from the flight of the ball what had occurred; if something had gone wrong they could check and remedy the cause. This knowledge will be invaluable to them when they are under pressure in important events.
>
> Several of the girls had persisted with faulty methods for some time and turned deaf ears to entreaties to become more orthodox in their ways. It is infuriating for the young to be told that they are doing something wrong and as a rule it is not until they have suffered disappointments by blowing up in the later stages of tournaments that they become amenable to advice.
>
> The girls who have had the benefit of Jacobs's coaching have

grasped how essential it is to work on orthodox lines and they have been persuaded to abandon some of their former faults. The girls seemed to learn more from working together than they might have done from individual tuition.

The idea of conducting this experiment arose after the 1960 Curtis Cup match at Lindrick, when British officials were impressed by the youth of the American team and the uniformity of methods employed by the American girls. The Ladies' Golf Union wasted no time in getting their training scheme under way. . . .

Today, when people consider the relative success of our Curtis Cup sides of the last few years, they point at once to the part played by the training set-up. For the purposes of the 1992 Curtis Cup at Hoylake, to give some indication of the present state of affairs, the players went over during the winter for group coaching from Bernard Gallacher who, in 1991, captained the European side in the Ryder Cup at Kiawah Island.

To return to Enid's disapproval of women becoming playing professionals, her reasons are entirely straightforward. 'They can't,' she says, 'play as well as men.'

In her view, today's amateurs would do well to count their blessings rather than contemplate how much greener the grass might be on the professional side of the fence.

'Amateur golf,' she contends, 'is a wonderful form of recreation in which you will meet people from all over the world. . . . You maybe won't see them again for years, but it is always the case that you can resume where you left off. . . . For myself, I've made a host of friends in playing and following the amateur game.'

That host, in turn, would say that their golfing lives had been vastly enriched by a champion who, over the years, attached so much more importance to other people's golf than ever she did to her own.

CHAPTER NINE

Cecil Leitch

Andra Kirkaldy, the famous St Andrews caddie, knew a thing or two
about golf on the distaff side of the game. After all, it was he who
had helped to hone the game of the first British Women's champion of
them all, Lady Margaret Scott.

When, in 1908, a sixteen-year-old by name of Cecil Leitch turned up
at St Andrews to play in the British Women's championship of that year,
Kirkaldy wasted no time in assessing the young woman with the plait
trailing half-way down her back. 'I followed her round,' noted Kirkaldy,
'and said afterwards that she would be lady champion one day.' Not only
that, but he added, unabashedly, that he had been sufficiently smitten by
her length and strength to hazard that she might one day win the men's
Amateur title.

Whilst in St Andrews, Cecil and her older sister, Edith, further came
under the scrutiny of the LGU secretary, Issette Pearson. Miss Pearson
recognised at once that the girls were richly gifted and, as they hailed from
Silloth in Cumbria, earmarked both for the England team. In Cecil's case,
as it turned out, that was not so easy, for the rule at that time stated that a
player should have a) English parents or b) have lived in England for
twenty years.

Since Cecil was the offspring of a Scottish doctor and, at that stage,
no more than eighteen years of age, Miss Pearson had to re-write her
rules. In truth, she went further still on Cecil's behalf. . . .Worried that
she was not getting the kind of match practice available to those who lived
in areas which had a county team, Miss Pearson called upon the country's
top men to take her under their wing.

Thus it was that she came to play that historic 72-hole match against
Harold Hilton at Walton Heath and Sunningdale in October 1910. In
accordance with Miss Pearson's instructions, Miss Leitch was in receipt of
a stroke on the even holes but none on the odd.

In front of a crowd of between three and four thousand, Miss
Leitch won at the penultimate hole, with her fourth round a gross 76 to
Hilton's 75.

In 1912, Cecil and all four of her sisters – Edith, May, Chris and

A picture from the scrapbook of the late Sir Henry Cotton. The triple Open Champion derived a great deal of satisfaction from playing and beating single-handed three of the leading women golfers in the world. From left to right: Enid Wilson, Mme René Lacoste, Joyce Wethered and Henry Cotton

Peggy – headed for the British Women's championship at Turnberry. As luck would have it, Peggy and Edith met in the first round, with Edith winning by 5 and 4 before bowing out to Miss Temple, the losing finalist. Cecil was in the other side of the draw where, en route to the semi-final, she had a one-hole win over May.

In the semi-final, she lost to Gladys Ravenscroft – a result which, at least in the eyes of one member of the press, was not entirely unexpected: 'It is whispered that Miss Cecil's temperament is not that of an ideal match-player and that, if things go wrong early in the game, she will have difficulty in recovering.'

By all accounts, the Silloth golfer began to press and went through a spell of 'hitting them on the napper', or, to you and me, topping.

Despite the question-mark hanging over her match-play, Cecil's overall game was by then such as to have the Ladies' Field of 25 October 1913 advocating that the handicapping system be adjusted: 'One of the things for which there will soon be a popular demand is the introduction of "plus" into the LGU system of handicapping. Of those players and officials who have really thought on this question, by far the greatest number are in favour of "plus". They realise that it would relieve the congestion on the scratch mark and put an end to many absurdities. . . .'

Cecil was duly the first to be given a plus handicap while, for the purposes of lifting her match-play on to a par with her Stroke-Play, she moved south and started playing for Hertfordshire and the Bushey Heath GC.

Both her method and her clubs excited much interest. She used the palm grip, with the right hand under the shaft for full shots. When it came to putting, she was given to overlapping with two fingers, rather than the usual one.

Enid Wilson, who described her as 'the first of the Amazons', was taken aback at the lack of padding in her grips. She also commented on the fact that the clubs were longer than your usual women's clubs, but lighter.

In 1914, Cecil did the double of English and British championships, her win in the British at Hunstanton having been predicted by one Hugh Leslie Dobree. 'Here is a player,' he wrote, 'who will literally revel in golf at Hunstanton. I can see her banging long iron shots over the hillocks, and she has just the sort of wrist stroke that will force the ball out of the exasperating marram grass which lines the fairway.' And so it came to pass, with Cecil defeating Miss Ravenscroft by two and one in the final.

It befell Bernard Darwin to sum things up in the pages of the following week's *Golf Illustrated*:

> I had not really watched Miss Leitch play since she won her famous victory over Mr Hilton some three years ago.
>
> She is a better player now than she was then and I sincerely pity the amateur who tries to give her a half [a stroke on every even hole] today. I do not know that her wooden club play is any better: indeed her style has rather deteriorated and she has a pronounced 'ducking' of the knees which, I think, forebodes disaster some day.
>
> Her iron club play, however, is really magnificent and as an all-round iron player she stands alone among the ladies. She hits the ball with a splendid firm snap, characteristic of a professional and she easily surpasses all her competitors in her power of playing a stroke with cut.
>
> The others are wonderfully accurate with their long iron shots, but the ball runs when it pitches. Miss Leitch is just as accurate and can make her ball bite the ground with fizz and stop.

After the war, Cecil carried on where she had left off, winning the English championship of 1919. So easily did she dispense with Mrs Temple Dobell, née Ravenscroft, in the 36-hole final that the ensuing newspaper coverage had to be padded out with details of an incident which had occurred at the seventeenth in a morning match in which Miss Leitch lost not a single hole.

> When the competitors went after their respective drives, Miss Leitch had been unable to find the ball they had been able to see quite clearly as they left the tee.
>
> 'Drop another, Cecil,' exhorted Mrs Dobell, who even went so far as to offer her a ball for that purpose.
>
> Miss Leitch proceeded to win the hole but the referee called a halt. Addressing the crowd, he asked if anyone had picked up a ball and, if so, would they please step forward.
>
> Then some man who should have known better – he was looking very shamefaced and uncomfortable – stepped forward and took the ball from his coat pocket. In a nervous voice he said, 'I am afraid I am the guilty person; I apologise most humbly.'

After that most uneasy of public confessions, Miss Leitch's winning of the hole was confirmed.

In 1920, 1921 and 1926, Cecil won her second, third and fourth British championships but by then she had a rival for the uppermost rung of the ladder in the person of Joyce Wethered. Miss Wethered made no secret of the fact that, despite her win over Cecil in the final of the 1920 English championship at Sheringham, she felt that Cecil was at that point far and away the better player. 'Had it been a question of playing long iron shots against Cecil it would have been a different story,' said Miss Wethered, in a reference to how short Sheringham had played in the week of her win. 'She stood in a class by herself in that department of the game, and it was due to her example that the prevailing belief amongst the opposite sex that ladies were incapable of hitting an iron shot effectively was at last dispelled.'

It was when they met at Prince's in 1922 that Miss Wethered recognised that she had put on length where Cecil, because of a troublesome arm injury, was shorter than she had been in 1920.

Miss Wethered confirmed her superiority by winning the 1922 instalment of the British, together with the 1924 and 1925 editions, not to mention her five successive English championships from 1920. Yet, in terms of their respective records, it has to be said that Miss Leitch would doubtless have had many more titles to her name had not her career been bisected by war.

Cecil's most satisfying win over Miss Wethered was probably in the final of the British at Turnberry in 1921. That was the week in which she had had an unforgettable first-round match against Alexa Stirling on a day when, she always vowed, conditions were a deal worse than those which had had tents and scores blowing sky high in the John Player Classic of 1973. 'And what you have got to remember,' she added, with feeling, 'was that in those days we didn't have anything in the way of waterproofs. We just got soaked to the skin.'

The severity of conditions was endorsed by Darwin who wrote of how he could not remember watching golf on a more unpleasant day and of how his report, on what became an ever soggier piece of paper, never made London.

'Miss Leitch,' he recalled, 'was in irresistible mood. I have a vision of her with her familiar bandeau and some kind of handkerchief knotted round her neck affronting the tempest and revelling in her defiance of it. The wide stance, the little duck of the right knee, the follow-through that sends the club through low as if boring its way through the wind – all the characteristic movements stand out in memory against the grey background.'

Cecil Leitch awkwardly placed

It was Miss Leitch's proud boast, towards the end of her life, that she had met all but one of those who won the British championship, an event which started in 1893. Also, she had vivid recollections of a dinner held for the LGU secretary, Issette Pearson, in 1911.

Quite definitely, she saw them as good old days, for she was appalled at the way in which golf, 1970s-style, could take between four and five hours a round. 'In my youth,' she recalled, 'we would get round Silloth in one hour and fifty minutes. We always had the same caddies who, like all good caddies, took the keenest interest in the game. They had only a few clubs to carry and, once putts had been holed, the club for the next tee shot was handed out and the caddies would then run forward to spot the balls and to be ready with the necessary club for the next shot.'

But, even if she did disapprove of such things as slow rounds and the early talk of a women's professional tour, she never lost her sense of humour. Mostly, she liked to relate stories against herself, her favourite being drawn from those years when, having retired from serious competition, she would play in the odd society event or open meeting.

On such an occasion, in truly wretched conditions, she contrived to return the winning score – a 76 which had the local golf correspondent reaching for the telephone with a story entitled '76 at 67'.

When, to his mingled fury and disbelief, his Cecil Leitch story never saw the light of day, the golf correspondent rang his sports editor for an explanation. 'That surely wasn't news,' said the sports editor, curtly. 'None of us here had ever heard of the fellow.'

CHAPTER TEN

Gloria Minoprio

Though the story goes that a Miss Beryl Hawtree, in a bid to win a long-driving contest at Portrush in 1911, smote the ball with such vigour that she fell flat on her back, women's golf in the Thirties was still a relatively genteel pastime.

On and off the course the golfers would converse politely amongst themselves – and none among them would consider flouting the conventional attire of shirt and skirt. As Gladys Ravenscroft, winner of the British and American championships of 1909, had once found to her cost, even the rolling up of a sleeve was likely to arouse adverse comment.

The English championship of 1933, when it got under way at Westward Ho!, was shaping in much the same way as any other championship of that time. That is until the hour drew nigh for the last match of the opening day, a game which was to involve Miss Nancy Halstead and one Miss Gloria Minoprio.

Miss Halstead, a popular figure in Surrey golf, was swinging in wait on the first tee and, at the same time, keeping a wary eye open for an opponent she had still to meet. The starter, meantime, was looking anxiously at his watch. Time was running out and, there being no sign of this Miss Minoprio, he called her name.

Normally, at such moments, a flustered competitor will come running from the clubhouse. What happened at Westward Ho! was that a large white car made a strikingly silent arrival in the car park. Out stepped a tall, slender figure dressed in dark navy cap, matching pullover and – horror of horrors, for it had never happened before – trousers.

Her face was white, her lips scarlet, her expression distant, Eleanor E. Helme of *The Morning Post* likening her to a stage Mephistopheles or executioner. Oblivious to the open-mouthed stares of those about her, Miss Minoprio walked straight to the tee, nodded in the direction of her opponent and hit her opening shot down the fairway.

The LGU women, when they had come round from the shock, talked angrily about the sheer irreverence of a player turning out in trousers. Indeed, they were sufficiently upset for their chairman to issue the following statement: 'I much regret that there should be this departure from the usual golfing costume at this championship.'

What Miss Minoprio was doing out on the course represented a still more amazing departure from the norm, for she was playing with but a single club, a straight-faced implement.

She had engaged a local caddie to carry a bag of spare balls and a duster, the latter to be used for polishing her club between shots. The said caddie was also under instruction to tee up Miss Minoprio's ball at each hole and, no doubt having the sense to realise that he was having an easy time of it, the good fellow took his role seriously.

Miss Minoprio talked not at all out on the links and, as Miss Halstead implied, it was an eerie experience. However, being a down-to-earth sort of creature, the Surrey girl realised that it would be madness to allow herself to be intimidated and duly won through at the fifteenth – at which point Miss Minoprio went straight to her car, never to be seen again all week. That legendary scribe, Henry Longhurst, captured her theatrical departure with a 'Sic transit Gloria'.

According to Enid Wilson in Donald Steel's *Bedside Book of Golf*, the hotels in Westward Ho!, Bideford and Barnstaple buzzed like beehives as the golfers expressed themselves on the subject of Miss Minoprio's disregard of convention.

'Today,' wrote Miss Wilson, 'Miss Minoprio's tactics would be dismissed instantly as the ingenuity of a master-mind behind a commercial concern wishing to promote something new in sports clothing. But in the 1930s such an idea was absurd because big business had not turned its attention to golf promotions.'

As it was, the possibilities they pondered were roughly as follows. Had Miss Minoprio been involved in some sort of wager? Had she been seeking publicity? Or, still more plausible, had it been a practical joke? With none of these suggestions supplying a satisfactory solution, Miss Minoprio's motives remained wrapped in mystery.

Twelve months later and she was among the starters for the English Women's championship at Seacroft where her first-round opponent was a Miss Betty Sommerville, a youngster making her first appearance in the championship. Miss Sommerville had been filled in as to what she might expect but, even so, was shaken beyond recall when the mystery figure materialised 'dressed as a stage demon' and carrying the one club.

'It was like playing a supernatural being,' Miss Sommerville explained to Miss Wilson. 'The effect was enhanced by Miss Minoprio's curious mannerism of waving the club to and fro above the ball instead of addressing it in the conventional manner.'

'Opponent Upset by "Fancy Dress"', ran the headline in the following day's *Daily Mail*. 'Our special correspondent,' as they called him, gave a vivid picture of Miss Minoprio's outfit, writing of 'tight-fitting,

Gloria Minoprio takes the stage at Westward Ho! Nancy Halstead is in pursuit

beautifully creased dark blue trousers, strapped under suede shoes to match; a pullover; a close-fitting blue hat; and gloves.'

If her attire was still seen as unorthodox, the same did not apply to her swing. Indeed, the chief question exercising the press that week was how good a player could she have been with a full set of equipment.

Having defeated Miss Sommerville by two and one, Miss Minoprio, in what represented one of her better tournament performances, lost in the next round to a Miss Mary Johnson, a fearless soul who went on to reach the final.

One player who had vivid memories of a match against Miss Minoprio was Miss Mary Holdsworth, a former president of the LGU. Shortly before her death, Miss Holdsworth recalled how Miss McFarlane, then president of the Union, had waited with her on the tee until Miss Minoprio made her entrance. 'We waited and waited – and suddenly, as always just in the nick of time, she appeared over the top of the sand dunes.'

Miss Holdsworth never forgot the white gloves Miss Minoprio wore that day. The thumb was cut out from one hand and from it there protruded a long, talon-like nail, painted red. 'Her eyes,' recalled Miss Holdsworth, 'were steely grey. Her hair was completely covered by her cap, though I have a suspicion that it was brown. Her features struck me as Grecian and I think everyone was agreed that she was a singularly good-looking woman.'

Having been exhorted by her friends to think positively, to remember that she had a bagful of clubs where her opponent only had the one, Miss Holdsworth forged into a four- and even five-hole lead. Miss Minoprio struck back, her wizardry with that one club wreaking havoc with Miss Holdsworth's nerves. 'She was keeping the ball down the middle – and when she was doing that, she was very effective. Her putts would jump a bit but they were well judged.'

They departed the eighteenth green all square and Miss Holdsworth remembered the deliberate effort she made to pull herself together before winning down the nineteenth. Miss Minoprio gave a slight murmur and departed whence she had come – over the sand dunes.

Miss Minoprio's last appearance in a major championship was in 1939 when, as has since been deduced, she was thirty-two.

Though presumed to have died during the war years, Miss Minoprio in fact married a Pole by name of Stefan Godlewska and ran a hotel in Vancouver before moving to Nassau where she died, from a rare blood disease, in March 1958.

She had always entered the championships from Littlestone but, when the tireless Enid Wilson tried to investigate her club career some years later, she was stymied by the fact that the club records, including the

Gloria Minoprio, an enigmatic force in the English Women's Championship of 1933 at Westward Ho!

handicap sheets, had been destroyed by fire in the mid–1940s. There were, though, one or two members who told of how they had often seen a lone figure, with an eye-catching swing, practising on the far reaches of the course. Rumour had it, they said, that she had been an amateur conjurer.

Here the story would have rested but for a Professor and Mrs Edwin A. Dawes who, on finding an old brochure advocating the skills of one Gloria Minoprio, the magician, substantiated these Littlestone rumours.

Professor Dawes, who in addition to all his academic qualifications, was a member of the Inner Magic Circle, had come across the booklet when delving into the historical aspects of magic in these islands. He and his wife, Amy, went on to learn how Graham Adams, one of the leading magicians of the Twenties and Thirties, had one day received a phone call from a man whose niece wanted to be taught magic. She, by all accounts, paid very handsomely for lessons from four different tutors to acquire conjuring skills. 'This,' explained Mrs Dawes 'is not the usual way for a woman – or, indeed a man – to acquire conjuring skills. These are usually learnt within a family from a parent or husband, or gradually self-taught from books and magic societies.'

Miss Minoprio's brochure, a most opulent production, was printed around 1935. It was well illustrated with her photographs and gave pages of information about her golfing prowess. In addition, there were details of the effects she performed and testimonials from her four teachers.

All her teachers died long ago but Professor and Mrs Dawes received a letter from one of the quartet, Les Levante, in which he said of Miss Minoprio, 'a more apt pupil I have yet to meet'.

Mrs Dawes included Gloria Minoprio in a talk she gave at a seminar at an International Brotherhood of Magicians' Convention in 1977. For all that, though, she conceded that the name Minoprio conjured up much the same mystery and intrigue among the magicians' fraternity as was the case in golfing circles.

'Miss Minoprio,' she added, 'generated a lot of interesting research but left a lot of questions unanswered.' Including, of course, that million dollar question as to whether or not she saw that single club as some kind of magic wand.

CHAPTER ELEVEN

Babe Zaharias

When Mildred 'Babe' Zaharias came to Britain for the 1947 British Women's championship at Gullane, it was because she had won everything there was to win in the States.

The daughter of Norwegian parents who had settled in Port Arthur on the Gulf of Mexico, the Babe excelled in basketball and athletics before trying her hand at golf. She won two gold medals – in the realms of hurdles and throwing the javelin – in the 1932 Olympics in Los Angeles. It would have been three but for the fact that the method she employed to win the high jump was the promptly outlawed Western Roll.

Where many would have spent the rest of their days dwelling on that seeming injustice, the Babe, as she was to demonstrate several times in a life cut short by cancer, was so extraordinarily gifted that she could take such setbacks in her stride.

It was on the day after the 1932 Olympics that she was taken to a golf course by Grantland Rice and Paul Gallico, two sportswriters fascinated to see if her talent would translate.

'Watching the Babe that day in early August, 1932,' wrote Rice, 'I thought I saw the makings of a champion – not in track and field where she already had proved her gold medal rating – but in golf, a sport where a girl might compete with men on their own terms. In my mind, she had all the physical attributes . . . wonderful legs, slender enough but strong . . . long-muscled arms . . . nice height and, above all, a pair of fine, strong hands and wrists.'

It was not too many outings later that the Babe decided that golf was the sport where her future lay and, in a bid to earn the necessary cash to work on her game, had a stint in show business. She would sing, play the harmonica, drive imitation golf balls and demonstrate different athletic skills.

The diversion was one she enjoyed, even if it had unfortunate repercussions. . . . When, after weeks of hitting practice shots to the point where she would have 'tape all over my hands and blood all over the tape', she won the 1935 Texas State Amateur, the USGA ruled that she was a professional. 'It seemed,' she explained, 'they'd had complaints from

A show of strength: Babe Zaharias in action at Wentworth in 1951

people who thought that because I'd done professional things with athletics, I didn't belong in amateur golf.'

In the spring of 1935, the Babe signed up with a sports company and set out on a highly-paid tour of exhibition matches with Gene Sarazen. There were two occasions when Joyce Wethered, making her well-documented visit to America as a professional, was on the opposing side. Though Miss Wethered each time had the better of the American, the Babe at that point was still in her formative golfing years, having little polish with which to complement her power.

But she learned much from Sarazen which was to stand her in good stead when, after marrying a wealthy wrestler by name of George Zaharias, she decided to ask for the return of her amateur status. Zaharias appreciated that he had married a competitor and, with a dearth of events available to women professionals at that juncture, felt that her place was back in the amateur game.

The USGA insisted that it would take three years. The Babe may have balked at the news but, far from moping, took up tennis and had lessons from Eleanor Tennant, coach to such as Alice Marble and Mo Connolly. She joined forces with Louise Brough with a view to entering the national doubles championship but, as had happened in golf, had her dreams shattered when tennis officialdom pronounced that they saw her as a professional.

From tennis she moved on to bowling – a sport in which she would one day give the most unexpected of barefoot demonstrations on the village bowling green during the course of the aforementioned British Women's championship at Gullane. But all the time she kept her hand in at golf, playing two or three practice rounds a week. She also participated, on an unpaid basis, in war-time exhibition games with players like Sam Snead and Bob Hope. The Babe, who was not without a sense of humour, prided herself on having made a good stooge for Hope, writing of the way in which he would tell spectators, 'There's only one thing wrong about Babe and myself. I hit the ball like a girl and she hits it like a man.'

On the same tack, she liked to recall a game in which she and Patty Berg took on Bing Crosby and Bob Hope at the San Gabriel Country Club: 'After I had knocked my opening tee shot 280 yards, Hope dropped to the ground and began beating on it with his hands and pretending to cry and wail. Bing put on an act of consoling Bob, then Bing took his drive. It was a good bit shorter than mine. So Bob started consoling Bing. . . .'

It was on 21 January 1943, that the Babe returned to golf's amateur arena. In 1945, for the first time since 1932 and the Olympics, she was picked as America's Woman Athlete of the Year. The citation read: 'Although Mrs Zaharias first won fame as a track star and later competed in most sports as an amateur and professional, she now concentrates on golf. It was in that field that she was outstanding during the '45 campaign.'

She had won the Western Open and the Texas Open, two tournaments which served as a prelude to a 1946 season in which she bagged five tournaments in a row, including her first American Amateur championship.

In 1947, she carried on where she had left off, bringing her tally of tournament wins to fifteen. At this, George Zaharias suggested she needed 'a win to top off your streak' and pointed her in the direction of the British Women's Open. Since her enthusiasm was dulled by the fact that her husband was unable to make the trip himself, it took Tommy Armour, the so-called 'Silver Scot' who was teaching at Medinah, to do the persuading.

'Mildred,' said Armour, after watching her belt a few balls over the cyclone fence at the end of his practice range, 'you go!'

It was an experience of which she was later to pen, 'I was to find that nothing I'd done in golf in the past was anything like playing this tournament. I've never had such an experience!'

The Babe arrived well in advance of the championship, booking into the Marine Hotel which is, today, a school for the Fire Department. Guy Robertson-Durham, the Gullane and Muirfield member who was to referee the Texan's first match and to this day lives on the road which runs at right-angles to Gullane's first fairway, will never forget the stir detonated by her arrival.

'There were crowds around her wherever she went. . . . Schoolchildren wanting her autograph and members of the press besieging her for interviews, so much so that she had virtually to barricade herself in her hotel room.'

The locals took pity on her, inviting her to their homes and, before too long, they began to enjoy each other's company. Mr Robertson-Durham tells of a day she was taken to Muirfield by Sam and Donald McIntosh, local golfing brothers. He can still hear Donald, on his return, saying, 'The person that beats the Babe will win.'

The McIntosh boys had been astounded by her length and, throughout East Lothian, tales grew of her extraordinary power. Indeed, it was because of the high level of interest that, when the day dawned for the start of the championship, Robertson-Durham was asked if he would referee the visitor's opening game versus Helen Nimmo. (Normally, referees were not employed until the later stages.)

Helen Nimmo, who had not played any golf of any consequence for five years because she had been in the army, can remember only too well how nervous she felt that day. 'It was obvious what was going to happen, but I did succeed in still being level at the turn.'

Miss Nimmo went on to lose at the fourteenth, but her abiding memory is of playing the bye and of the way in which the Babe caught the green in two at the fifteenth. 'For the rest of us,' said Miss Nimmo, who now resides in Edinburgh, 'the hole asked for two woods and another shot besides. Yet, on that day, the Babe followed what was, for her, a pretty poor drive by whacking a one-iron up the hill and on to the green. It was far and away the longest one-iron I have ever seen.'

Enid Wilson's account of the championship follows, but mention must first be made of how, for all that the Babe was as extrovert as the majority of her rivals were reserved, most took her to their hearts.

Robertson-Durham, talking of the Highland Fling she danced after defeating Jean Donald in the semi-final, reports that Jean Donald took it in the best of spirits. Again, there had been nothing but wide-eyed astonishment and admiration when, in an exhibition match involving Robertson-Durham, Jean Donald, Helen Holm and the Babe on the day after the championship, the Babe departed Gleneagles' fifteenth tee by means of a standing somersault.

In a bid to win over any remaining sceptics, if there were any, Frank Moran was moved to re-examine her approach in a piece which appeared in *The Scotsman* in the week following the championship: 'By our standards Mrs Zaharias was undoubtedly unconventional, having a touch of showmanship and revelling in crowds. All that should be understandable when we remember that she has been in the public eye as an athlete since she was a youngster and that she toured as co-exhibitioner with Byron Nelson, Horton Smith, and other men stars of American golf. She also has high spirits and a sense of humour, and she could very readily switch her set-jaw, robot expression that went with an almost sinister concentration when she sized up the surface of the green, to a broad smile and a bit of chaff thrown in.'

Moran's first impressions were in keeping with how she has always been seen by the American golf-writing fraternity. Blackie Sherrod, of the Dallas *Morning News*, has described her as 'charming in her looseness and relaxed naturalness and great good nature. Most sports celebrities, some without realizing, immediately assume some sort of pose when speaking with media. . . .But not Babe. In forty years of this dodge, I've seen only a handful of jocks with that freewheeling ease in interviews. Abe Lemmons, the basketball coach, was one. Roy Campanella, the catcher, was another. Don Meredith came close. Johnny Miller, the golfer, and Magic Johnson. But Ms. Babe wrote the book.'

Sherrod went on to say that the awe he felt for the Babe grew on him after he had had time to reflect and appreciate the extent of her naturalness: 'Not her accomplishments, not her reputation nor her history, but her downhome personality.'

Gullane made her an honorary member, but still more significant was the fact that all the crack male amateurs in the area had been prepared to accept that she was a match for any of them.

'She was certainly as long as a top amateur – and damned nearly as long as a professional,' says Robertson-Durham. He did not mind admitting how, even in his hey-day, his clubbing at the fifteenth, the hole where the Babe used a one-iron for her second against Miss Nimmo but a four-iron when playing Bunty Stephens, had always been a toss-up between a spoon and a three-iron.

Men came from all parts to see if she was as long as everyone said and, confirmed Robertson-Durham, they went away shaking their heads in bewilderment and agreeing that she most certainly was.

The Babe was the talk of the club for years to come, with Robertson-Durham gleefully illustrating the point with the story of how the then secretary of Gullane, a Lt Col. W. H. Pike, could for months afterwards be spotted going about the club clutching a tennis ball in either hand.

This strange activity was, as you will have guessed, as a result of a tip he had received from the Babe on how best to strengthen his wrists.

The following is an excerpt from a piece written by Enid Wilson for Donald Steel's *Golfer's Bedside Book* in 1965. Of all the articles written by Miss Wilson in her forty years as a golf writer, this was the one which, she felt, detonated the most interest.

The British Championship of 1947

When 'The Babe' arrived at Gullane early in June, there was still evidence of the exceptionally severe winter. The frost had not worked out of the ground, so the top surface was unusually soft and heavy. These conditions suited her admirably, and the tremendous carry of her drives was utterly disconcerting to her opponents, for she often out-hit them by 100 yards from the tee. An instance of her power came in her match with Miss Frances Stephens when, on the 540-yard fifteenth hole, 'Babe's' second shot with a four-iron pitched over the back of the green.

Although we did not know it at the time, 'Babe' was the first of the atomic and jet age women strikers of the ball. She stood straight up and with squared stance delivered all the might she could muster. Her only mannerism was the curious one of licking the thumb of the glove on her left hand, which she then wiped on the slate-blue corduroy slacks which she wore throughout the championship. Her swing was too forceful to be pretty, and many of her strokes finished way off line. When they did so, it mattered not, for she had the strength to get home with her seconds from almost any position. After the grounding she had received in her early days from Sarazen, bunkers held no terrors for her and, although she frequently missed the greens at the short holes, she rarely missed getting threes, the excellence of her recoveries being equalled by her ability to hole out.

The Home Internationals were held at Gullane in the week prior to the championship and 'The Babe' was an interested spectator. They gave her a chance of seeing and measuring the calibre of her future opponents. She followed a match in which one of the players holed out with a full seven-iron and the small gallery expressed their appreciation of that approach with silent awe. 'The Babe' was amazed by their behaviour and, in tones of bewilderment, addressed a bystander, 'Don't people here applaud a good stroke?' It was then explained to her that the absence of outward emotion was a sign of respect.

Some days later, after 'The Babe' had inflicted a severe defeat on her antagonist and they were faced with a long walk back to the clubhouse, she suggested that they might play in, and this they proceeded to do. By way of entertaining the gallery, 'The Babe' started playing trick shots, but the effect was not what she had anticipated and the crowd melted away. They had come to see golf, not showmanship, but that was something she could not understand.

The main road from Edinburgh to North Berwick runs through Gullane and the first tee of Gullane's Number One Course is close to where the road bends at the beginning of the village street. The tee is surrounded by a fence of white posts with a top rail on which the natives like to lean and watch the players driving off. 'The Babe's' custom was to walk down to the course from the hotel at the far end of the village and to vault lightly over the top rail on to the teeing ground. She did this without any perceptible effort, and to the considerable amazement of whoever happened to be standing there at the time.

Having spent so much of her life travelling, 'The Babe' was in no way disconcerted by having to play on a type of course that she had not seen before. She was supremely confident of winning and buoyed by her unbroken run of successes over the past year. Moreover, she told the reporters that she had played and beaten (without the aid of strokes) every member of the American Walker Cup team.

She came to Britain at a time when the austerities of the war were still prevailing, and when the older players were past their zenith, and the up-and-coming generation still seeking to find their feet. Miss Pam Barton was one who would have stood up to 'The Babe' without flinching but, alas, she had been killed in a flying accident whilst serving with the WAAF at Manston.

Miss Helen Nimmo, a member of Gullane, was the American's opponent in the first round of the championship and 'The Babe' beat her by five and four. She then met Mrs Sheppard, a sturdy Midlander and English international with a good record in match events, but Mrs Sheppard's courage and fine short game were of no avail against 'The Babe' who beat her by four and two. In the third round, an ex-Irish champion, Mrs Val Reddan, who had represented Britain in the Curtis Cup at the Essex Country Club, Massachusetts, in 1938, and came away with two points, was hammered by the visitor by six and four. Another Scot, one who had represented her country, and also Britain against France, Mrs Cosmo Falconer, fared slightly worse, losing by six and five. Thus 'The Babe' had accounted for four highly experienced golfers in the early stages of the championship and fortune then decreed that her remaining opponents should be young ones.

In the fifth round she had her hardest match of the week, and that was with Miss Frances Stephens, whose seeming frailty then made people wonder if she would have the stamina to stay in big golf. The slender Lancashire girl stuck doggedly with 'The Babe' for twelve holes, and then might prevailed by three and two.

'The Babe' was through to the semi-finals and there confronted the Scottish champion, Miss Jean Donald, daughter of a local doctor. All Edinburgh and the East of Scotland had been anticipating and waiting for this meeting of champions but, although 'The Babe' revelled in the size of the crowd, and was inspired by it, the effect on Miss Donald was not so good and she began by taking three putts. Then the American had birdies on the second, third and fourth – and romped away to win by seven and five, her score that afternoon being five under fours.

Meanwhile, a strong, determined player from Middlesex, Miss Jacqueline Gordon, had been making her way through the other half of the draw, and thereby vindicating her selection in the English team the previous week.

Miss Gordon was not in the least intimidated by her foe that day and started well by playing the first nine in 36, one under par. A birdie on the eleventh enabled her to lead 'The Babe' by two holes, but by the end of the morning round they were all square, both players having gone round in 75. When they resumed, Miss Gordon faltered on the first hole. 'The Babe' grasped the initiative and delivered a mortal thrust with an eagle three at the second. Then, when the English girl slipped again on the third, it was apparent that the championship was going to America. Miss Gordon did her best, but the situation was hopeless and 'The Babe' ultimately triumphed by five and four.

On her return to the United States, 'The Babe' received such tempting offers she was prevailed upon to turn professional again.

Maybe the sands had started to run out, for not long afterwards she was troubled by a pain in her left side. The greatest of her victories was the American Women's Open championship she won at Peabody, Massachusetts, in 1954. ('The Babe' finished twelve strokes ahead of her nearest rival, Betty Hicks.) The previous summer she had endured a colostomy, and so commenced the fight against an enemy to which all human flesh is defenceless in the end.

Note: Over Christmas, 1955, when the Babe was dying in hospital, she asked to see a golf course 'one more time'. They took her to the Colonial Club where she walked across the first fairway before bending down to touch the green. That frail, farewell gesture may have been at the other end of the spectrum to the Babe in full golfing cry, but it was one which told how her love of the game was no less full-blooded than her play.

From Taylor on Golf

Regarding the playing of the game, a curious contrast is offered between *la belle Americaine* and her English sister. During the course of my visit to the United States I secured an opportunity of seeing a little of the American Championship for Ladies and I was enabled to watch a few of the best lady players performing during the run of the competition.

On this showing I have not the slightest hesitation in saying the American lady player is not at the present time in the same class as the British, considering the best of the latter as compared with the best of the former. As an excuse for the American ladies, however, it is only common fairness to say they have only taken up the game very recently, but in the course of a few years' time the country should be capable of producing a team of players that would possess a fair chance of winning on this side of the Atlantic. . . .

And there is one thing to be said about the lady golfer in America. She takes up the game in a thoroughly practical and business-like manner; there is no half-heartedness displayed in her style. With the sleeves of her jersey or blouse rolled up, she attacks golf in a workman-like manner. This wonderful keenness – I can describe it in no other way – must have its effect upon the game, and in the natural sequence of events they will, beyond a doubt, come rapidly to the front.

J. H. TAYLOR, 1902

CHAPTER TWELVE

The Curtis Cup

Margaret and Harriot Curtis, who were destined to compete in the 1907 final of the US Women's Amateur championship at the Midlothian Country Club, were so captivated by the impromptu match held between the various American visitors and home players at the 1905 British Women's championship at Cromer that they began to dream of an official fixture involving the two lands.

For long years these celebrated sisters allowed that dream to percolate. . . . They were heartened by another informal clash – 'America versus the Colonies' held at Portrush in 1911 – and still more so by a third such match, at Sunningdale in 1930.

Joyce Wethered was called upon to captain the 1930 British team but, though she would agree to take charge in 1932 on the occasion of the first official contest, the former English and British champion was not in a position to accept the captaincy for Sunningdale.

Molly Gourlay, who was awarded the OBE for a distinguished wartime career and who died in 1990 at the age of ninety-two, took her place. Miss Gourlay who, like Miss Wethered, hailed from Surrey, at that time had two English championships to her name, together with an enviably panoramic feel for the game.

This future chairman of England and the LGU, not to mention instigator of the Commonwealth tournament, succeeded in choosing a side which beat the Americans with room to spare. Nor did her golf suffer in the process, for her own result – she defeated Glenna Collett Vare – was the most impressive of them all.

So healthy were the crowd figures – five thousand, according to Miss Gourlay – and so intense the interest from the press, that all were convinced the time was at last ripe for a more formal contest.

Thus it was that Margaret and Harriot Curtis, the former of whom won the US Amateur title on three occasions and was still playing in the championship at the age of sixty-five, presented a simple, silver trophy, 'To stimulate friendly rivalry among the women golfers of many lands.'

The Curtis sisters offered to replace the Cup with a more regal version in 1958 but this was refused on sentimental grounds. As, indeed,

The 1905 British Championship at Cromer attracted enough American visitors to make possible the first unofficial match between the women golfers of the new world and the old

The British team which played an informal match against America and the Colonies at Royal Portrush in 1911. The homeside won 7–2

was a later suggestion that the Curtis Cup follow the example of the Ryder Cup in becoming an America versus Europe affair. The original terms of reference would seem to have allowed for more countries getting involved but, even when the United States was trouncing Great Britain and Ireland with scorelines bordering on the embarrassing, there were American voices which insisted that nothing be changed. They liked the match as it was.

Down the years, that 'friendly rivalry' has led to lasting friendships and memories to outshine even the most glittering prizes on the professional circuit.

'For me,' said Nancy Lopez, the most charismatic woman professional of them all, 'the Curtis Cup added a new dimension to the game. . . . I was seventeen when I played in 1976 at Royal Lytham and St Anne's and I was spellbound. . . . There was this wonderful sense of tradition; a feeling associated with the Curtis Cup itself, the course and the country. It was my first time representing America and my first time in England. To this day, my spine tingles at the memory.'

As for Laura Davies, she will tell you that nothing she has achieved as a professional has bettered that moment when she holed downhill from ten feet on the last green to defeat Anne Sander in the Muirfield match of

Molly Gourlay (left) and Diana Fishwick in the final of the 1929 English Women's Championship which was won by Miss Gourlay

133

*The first Great Britain and Ireland Curtis Cup side, 1932. Front row (from left to right):
Mrs J. B. Watson, Miss Doris Park, Miss Molly Gourlay Back row (from left to right):
Miss Enid Wilson, Miss Wanda Morgan, Miss Joyce Wethered (captain), Miss Diana
Fishwick, Miss Elsie Corlett*

1984: 'I can still hear the claps and congratulations from the rest of the
Great Britain and Ireland side ringing in my ears. . . .'

But no one, perhaps, has captured the unique atmosphere better than
did Vicki Goetze, who participated in the 1990 match at Somerset Hills
when she was no more than seventeen years of age.

'It was', said Vicki, 'a truly great feeling playing for my country.
When Anne Sander and I were waiting for the starter's call on the first
morning, I felt more nervous than I have ever felt in my life – and I didn't
even have to hit the tee-shot!'

THE THIRTIES

'To England, in May, 1932, came Miss Marion Hollins with the pick of
the Americans. They settled in at the Great Fosters Hotel and, to the mild
astonishment of the locals, they were to be seen practising foursomes
morning and afternoon.'

So wrote Enid Wilson, who had been chosen for Great Britain and Ireland's first official Curtis Cup side. 'Scotch foursomes,' she continued, 'are never played in America and Miss Hollins insisted on her side playing in every possible combination, in order to find the best pairings for her team when they met us. . . . The British team assembled the day before the match at Wentworth, having been asked to be there in time for tea. Most of them knew the course and the necessity for a trial spin in the foursomes had not occurred to anyone.'

Joyce Wethered, the British captain, has recalled how she and Marion Hollins seemed equally aghast at each other's pairings for the foursomes when they exchanged lists: 'We had both much too ingeniously predicted something quite different for the opposite side.

'As events were to prove,' she continued, ruefully, 'Marion Hollins certainly made the wiser choice.'

The Americans won each of the three foursomes. The host team came back at them in the afternoon, with Joyce Wethered, Enid Wilson and Diana Fishwick notching points from the singles, but the overall result was 5½–3½ in America's favour.

In 1934, at Chevy Chase, Maryland, the British succeeded in sharing the foursomes, only to lose all but one of the singles and allow the Americans to stretch their winning margin of 1932 to 6½–2½. But there was never any question of a runaway win in the wet and heavy conditions at Gleneagles in 1936. This was the match in which Jessie Valentine, making the first of her seven Curtis Cup appearances, holed across the home green to beat Mrs L. D. Cheney and enable Great Britain and Ireland to share the day.

The fourth Curtis Cup was held at the Essex Country Club, Massachusetts, home club of the Curtis sisters. Here, for the first time, the Great Britain and Ireland side had the better of the foursomes but, crucially, lost five of the six singles.

1948

After a break of ten years, the match was held at Birkdale. America won 6½–2½ but Louise Suggs, from the ranks of the visiting team, was to remember the occasion more for an incident in her halved match with Philomena Garvey.

Having won each of the seventeenth and eighteenth to draw level, Miss Suggs had stalked across to the first tee, only to have her captain, Glenna Collett Vare, yelling after her that Curtis Cup matches did not go to the nineteenth.

'It was all so embarrassing,' said Miss Suggs. 'I would never knowingly have put a foot out of line.'

Elizabeth Price-Fisher and Bunty Stephens, Curtis Cup heroines of the 1950s

1954 Curtis Cup side (from left to right): Miss Ruth Peel, Miss Elizabeth Price, Mrs Jessie Valentine, Mrs John Beck (captain), Miss Janette Robertson, Miss Frances Stephens, Miss Jeanne Bisgood

Off the course, Miss Suggs remembers how startled the Americans were at the state of post-war Britain: 'There was scaffolding everywhere. We thought we were deprived but our discomfort had been as nothing to that of the folks we met in the North of England.'

Uncomfortably aware of the fact that the British players' equipment was well past its best, several members of the American Curtis Cup contingent handed across their clubs before returning home.

THE FIFTIES

Great Britain and Ireland's first win, at Muirfield in 1952, followed their heaviest defeat in six starts – 7½–1½ at Buffalo in 1950. Frances Stephens, or 'Bunty', as she was always known, had had most to do with saving a whitewash at Buffalo and was again in inspired form in Scotland. She won one of the singles points, with Jeanne Bisgood and Elizabeth Price bagging the other two. Elizabeth's match with Grace de Moss was the game which would decide the result.

One up coming to the thirteenth and still one up with five to play, Elizabeth, whose achievements were all the more impressive in that she was suffering from diabetes, pulled her drive at the fourteenth into a bunker whereas her opponent hit straight up the fairway. The home player came out well, but her ball flopped into sand for a second time.

'It will take a socket to save us now,' said a well-known amateur who was standing beside the green as Miss de Moss stood to her third, a seemingly straightforward pitch.

'No sooner were the words out of his mouth,' wrote the late Tom Scott, 'than Miss de Moss executed a socket which will for all time be immortal. The ball flew off the club at right angles into long rough.'

The American had one hurried and ineffectual stab at the ball in the long grass before perpetrating 'the mother and father of all sockets, one which flew off at an even greater angle than the first. The crowd looked on in silent sympathy. Miss de Moss had now played five against our girl's four and had still to reach the green. This she did with her next shot, but Miss Price was calm and won the hole with ease. So ended one of the most dramatic holes ever played in international golf.'

Two up with four to play instead of all square, Elizabeth, who followed Enid Wilson as the *Daily Telegraph*'s women's golf correspondent, won the fifteenth to draw three ahead and then clinched the Curtis Cup for Britain when she laid a curling, downhill putt stone dead at the short sixteenth.

The British lost at Merion in 1954, but regained the Cup at Prince's in 1956. After losing two of the three foursomes, Jessie Valentine, Angela Ward (later Mrs Michael Bonallack) and Elizabeth Price had emphatic singles wins. All of this set the stage for a thrilling climax involving Frances Smith (Stephens) and Polly Riley, whose Curtis Cup records for singles were at that point identical. . . . Played four, won four.

'The suspense,' wrote Enid Wilson, 'was prolonged to the thirty-sixth green, where the home player hit a glorious shot to the flag after the American's approach had faded and fallen short.'

The Riley–Smith finale was repeated at Brae Burn in 1958 when, with the latter extending her unbeaten singles run, Great Britain and Ireland succeeded in halving the match and clinging to the trophy. This was something that no visiting team – Ryder, Walker or Curtis – had ever previously accomplished.

The individual tallies of Frances Smith and Elizabeth Price, both of whom played in every match from 1950 to 1960, tell as much as anything about Great Britain and Ireland's success in the Fifties. Smith's final record, inclusive of foursomes, was – played eleven, won seven, halved one, and Price's record was – played twelve, won seven, halved one.

THE SIXTIES AND SEVENTIES

Just as the British had shone in the Fifties, so the Sixties and Seventies belonged to the Americans – exclusively as it turned out. . . .

The period opened with a 6½–2½ win for the Americans at Lindrick where England's Ruth Porter won the only singles point and the home team was captained by the great-hearted Maureen Garrett, whose contribution to the goodwill element of the match has over the years been such that she was in 1983 the recipient of the USGA's Bobby Jones award.

1964 Curtis Cup side, Royal Porthcawl.
Back row (from left to right): Julia Greenhalgh, Sheila Vaughan, Susan Armitage, Bridget Jackson. Front row (from left to right): Ruth Porter, Marley Spearman, Elsie Corlett (captain), Angela Bonallack, Joan Lawrence

A trio of Curtis Cup golfers. All three – Ruth Slark, née Porter, Bridget Jackson and Marley Harris, formerly Spearman – played in the match three times

One-sided the 1960 match may have been but, to the enfabled JoAnne Carner, it was a contest which afforded recollections which, to this day, have her laughing out loud.

Judith Ella, a player with a keen sense of mischief who was making her one and only appearance in the American side, took it upon herself to

Angela Bonallack, née Ward. Wife of the R & A Secretary, Michael Bonallack and a double English champion who played in six Curtis Cups

Mickey Walker shaking hands with her manager, Mark McCormack, as she embarks on a professional career. Twice a winner of the British Women's Championship, Mickey captained Europe on the occasion of the first Solheim Cup

tell the British players that the Americans had been invited to meet the Queen on the Monday after the match.

'The British,' recalled Carner, in reminiscing at a recent Nabisco Dinah Shore championship at Palm Springs, 'could not understand why they had not been invited and made no secret of the fact that they were more than a little hurt. But still they went out of their way to be helpful in the matter of teaching us how to curtsey.' Only when they had finally mastered the technique did the visitors gleefully admit to having had no such royal invitation.

In terms of golfing technique, it was Mrs Carner's impression that the Americans were ahead of their British counterparts at this stage. Though she deemed Angela Bonallack, against whom she had three epic singles matches, in a class of her own – 'the best I ever met' – as a competitor, she felt that none of the British players had a particularly solid swing: 'All of them were always up on their toes.'

Anne Sander, in analysing the American superiority of the Sixties and Seventies, felt that it had much to do with the way in which the American teams of those days would consist of players such as JoAnne Carner and herself who would participate in match after match and thus fall easily into the foursomes format. By way of elaborating, she noted how, in the Sixties, only three players, from a total of five teams, had turned professional. Again, in the Seventies, that figure was no higher than eight.

If, collectively, the British were at sea over that period, there were yet some admirable individual records. For example, Ruth Porter's performance in winning three matches, losing three and halving one was eminently praiseworthy. This tiny, three-times winner of the English

Dinah Henson, née Oxley, winner of the 1970 British Women's Championship at Gullane

American Curtis Cup side of 1976, Royal Lytham, St Anne's. From left to right:
Barbara McIntire (captain), Donna Horton, Nancy Syms, Nancy Lopez, Cynthia Hill,
Deborah Massey, Carol Semple, Beth Daniel, Barbara Barrow

Great Britain & Ireland Curtis Cup side of 1976, Royal Lytham, St Anne's. From left
to right: Belle Robertson MBE (captain), Ann Irvin, Anne Stant, Jenny Lee Smith,
Suzanne Cadden, Julia Greenhalgh, Tegwen Perkins, Dinah Henson, Mary McKenna

championship was always having to compensate for her lack of length off the tee. This she did by bisecting every fairway and polishing her short-game until it was virtually watertight.

In the 1964 match at Royal Porthcawl, Marley Harris snatched two half points from the singles and, along with Angela Bonallack, won both her foursomes. (Mrs Bonallack, though she so often suffered at the hands of JoAnne Carner in the singles, won four of her five Curtis Cup foursomes.)

Four years later, at Royal County Down, Ann Irvin did much to ease the disappointment of Great Britain and Ireland's loss by winning both her singles at the top of the line-up. This endlessly reliable competitor joined forces with Belle Robertson to defeat Anne Welts (Sander) and Shelley Hamlin in the first foursomes series – and went on to beat first Welts and then Hamlin in the singles. As for the second foursome, Ann and Belle escaped with half a point from their match with Mary Lou Dill and Peggy Conley.

Mickey Walker's performance in the 1972 match at Western Gailes was along much the same impressive lines. Mickey, who won the British Women's championship in 1971 and 1972 and who was chosen to captain Europe's leading women professionals in the inaugural Solheim Cup at

Dinah Henson, née Oxley, watching Vivien Saunders who, since turning professional in 1969, has taught countless top squads and individuals at her own club, Abbotsley

Diane Bailey, who captained the winning Curtis Cup sides of 1986 and 1988

Lake Nona in 1990, collected three and a half points out of four on that occasion.

In tandem with Mary McKenna, she won both her foursomes while, in the singles, she had a halved match with Laura Baugh, a *Golf Digest* 'Most Beautiful Golfer of the Year', before defeating Jane Booth.

Although Dinah Henson, whose record in English and British championships had been on a par with Mickey Walker's, was seldom seen at her glorious best in the context of a Curtis Cup, the Surrey golfer netted two points at Lytham in 1976, having the better of Cindy Hill in the first singles series and linking with Tegwen Perkins of Wales to defeat Carol Semple and Nancy Roth Syms.

THE EIGHTIES

By winning the first two matches of this decade, the Americans clocked up thirteen consecutive wins. But the match at Muirfield in 1984 was the closest since the tie of 1958, with the Americans winning by no more than

9½ to 8½. That closeness was mirrored in the warmth of the reception given to Molly Gourlay.

Advancing years had left the elderly Surrey stalwart decidedly unsteady on her feet, but she stood for thirty minutes at the closing dinner; her talk on the spirit of the match in its earliest days reducing tough young players to tears.

Diane Bailey MBE, the captain, was much heartened by that 1984 result and, in 1986, headed for Prairie Dunes with a team which very definitely had the feeling they could win.

Though all the players felt that way, Belle Robertson who, at fifty, was playing in her seventh Curtis Cup, can remember being 'very British' in a radio interview at the end of a first day which saw Great Britain and Ireland leading 6½–2½: 'Instead of talking of a possible win for our side, I simply concentrated on the fact that there was still a long way to go.'

In doing her homework, Diane Bailey had examined the poor starts

The winning Great Britain and Ireland side at the 1988 Curtis Cup at Royal St George's. Back row (left to right): Claire Hourihane, Karen Davies, Jill Thornhill, Sue Shapcott, Vicki Thomas. Front row (left to right): Julie Hall, née Wade, Elizabeth Boatman (vice-captain), Diane Bailey (captain), Linda Bayman, Shirley Huggan, née Lawson

British players had made down the years, her calculations revealing how a nadir had been reached in 1982 at Denver when player after player lost the first hole. As a result, she had impressed on this 1986 team how vital it was that they should get off on the right foot.

At Prairie Dunes, to her immense satisfaction, the Great Britain and Ireland side won the first hole or halved it in every game. When Belle and Mary McKenna halved the third foursome on the second morning, it meant that whatever happened in the afternoon, the British could not lose.

'Mercifully,' recalls Belle, in her autobiography, 'we stayed in control at Prairie Dunes, with Trish Johnson holing the putt that enabled us to do what no British team had ever done before. To wit, win on American soil.'

Trish Johnson's contribution that week was an outstanding four points out of four, but what did most to contribute to the team's unadulterated delight was the fact that every member of the side had had a hand in amassing the thirteen points.

Still more was done to redress the balance when the British, again under the excellent captaincy of Diane Bailey, won again at Royal St George's in 1988, with the scoreline 11–7. Enid Wilson, who had played in the first match in 1932, took no time at all to assess the difference between this team and British teams of the past.

Having watched as Sue Shapcott and Karen Davies defeated Cindy Schofield and Carol Thompson on a first morning when the British took a 2½–½ lead, Miss Wilson said that she had never expected to live to see the day when British girls outplayed Americans on and around the greens. 'Our two,' said the old champion, 'pitched and putted like angels.'

Linda Bayman, whose garden backs on to the course, holed for an eagle from off the first green to halve the top singles with Tracy Kerdyk. The roar which greeted the local player's three carried across the links, whipping up still more excitement and paving the way for the British side to bed down with a 6–3 lead.

On the second day, a wickedly chilly one as it turned out, the British won the foursomes 2–1 before clinching the match with singles won by Sue Shapcott, who claimed three points over the two days, Vicki Thomas and Linda Bayman.

Jill Thornhill, whose third and final match this was, had picked up two and a half points that week, but still more striking was her haul, over three Curtis Cups, of six wins and four halves in twelve starts.

No one was better qualified than Jill Thornhill to captain the next side and, typically, the Surrey player did everything she could by way of preparing for the return match at Somerset Hills, New Jersey.

Only by now, the Americans were desperate to retrieve the trophy. In 1986 they had made the mistake of having eight newcomers in their team. Such seasoned campaigners as Carol Semple Thompson, Pat Cornett and Leslie Shannon were included in their side for Royal St George's in 1988 and, though such a move did not stop a second successive British win, the USGA felt confident they were back on the right lines.

In 1990, the Americans not only achieved the right blend in terms of personnel but put in a deal of behind-the-scenes practice. Without doubt, their most lethal weapon in the foursomes was the combination of the fifty-two-year-old Anne Sander, playing in her eighth Curtis Cup, and the seventeen-year-old Vicki Goetze. Leslie Shannon, the American captain, made laughing references to how one of the pair was complaining of hot flushes and the other, toothache, but the two added up to an unbeatable partnership. They won the first point of the first morning against Helen Dobson and Catriona Lambert. Then, on the second day, they accounted for Julie Hall and Kathryn Imrie.

Though the Americans won 14–4, there was a singles result for Julie Hall to set alongside her best, with the result in question a win over Vicki Goetze at the start of the first afternoon. What with a foursomes win on the first morning, Julie was able to salvage a respectable total of two points from the overall drubbing.

Vicki Thomas picked up a point through defeating Carol Semple Thompson in the sixth single of the first day, while the other win belonged to Catriona Lambert and Helen Dobson as they made amends for their first-day loss by defeating Karen Noble and Margaret Platt.

To set alongside her foursomes win, Lambert was the recipient of some warm words from Maureen Orcutt, who had played in the unofficial Curtis Cup of 1930 and in all the official matches throughout the Thirties. At eighty-three, this grand old golfer was still in practice and the holder of her club championship.

'That girl,' said she, pointing to Catriona, 'stands to the ball quite beautifully. She has the look of a champion.'

High praise indeed, and enough to have the Scot walking tall into the 1992 instalment of this great match at Hoylake.

From a Curtis Cup Diary
by Elaine Farquharson

SOMERSET HILLS 1990,

AMERICA 14 — GREAT BRITAIN AND IRELAND 4

Saturday 21 July
. . . Lunch, then it's off to Somerset Hills. It's very muggy so we only hit a few shots and putt a little. The course looks very lush and tree-lined. The putting green is amazing – uphill it's like a shag pile carpet; downhill it's like glass.

Sunday 22
. . . The fruit here is gorgeous and there's bagels, bacon, sausage, potatoes, salad, ham, waffles, muffins, etc., etc. Arrive at club and everyone gets weighed before they hit balls. Caddie draw is done and mine is Frank Buchanan, whose relatives come from Scotland. He has caddied here every summer for six years. Catriona [Lambert] lands Jim, a dealer on Wall Street.

The course is very lush and all about position off the tee and then hitting into the right side of the pin. Greens are slower than the putting green. It's very hot playing and we're constantly reminded to wear our hats, to have wet towels about our backs and to drink plenty.

The back nine is the tougher with a lot of dog-legs and this is what we're going to concentrate on tomorrow.

Into the changing rooms and another weigh-in. . . . I lost one pound, which is OK as I have plenty in reserve. Kathryn [Imrie] loses three pounds and is told to drink more. This is a little strange because she should be used to these conditions after having been at university in Arizona.

A decidedly sticky team pile into the bus and head for home and the showers.

Monday 23
Tonight we're going to a restaurant with the US team. . . . The meal was

fun. I was sitting between Karen Noble and Robin Weiss and opposite Margaret Platt. Everyone is mixing really well. Perhaps it's easier than, for example, the European team championships where there are so many different sides that it's impossible to mix.

Tuesday 24
Today it's quite cool to start eighteen holes – front nine just practice; back nine medal. As soon as you have a card in your hand you go into all the places you shouldn't be. As usual, you always think you've done worse than everyone else but, as it turns out, most of us score over par. We get our knuckles rapped. From now on we've to think par golf (or better).

Wednesday 25
Today it's eighteen holes counting fairways and pars. It's the first day without clouds, but it's not humid – more like the Continent.

I feel more confident with my swing and start well although a couple of times I pitch close but miss the putt. I actually hit the third in two and then three putt.

Linzi [Fletcher] is upset/annoyed because she was told at lunch she would not be playing foursomes. She's experiencing all the emotions I've had at Scottish level and British [Vagliano Trophy]. You think, 'What do I have to do – Why me?' So the pairings are Helen Dobson and Catriona Lambert; Julie Hall and Kathryn Imrie; and Helen Wadsworth and myself.

Picnic at Golf House [HQ of the USGA] for the opening of the Golfing Girl exhibition. There is a splendid Ben Hogan display with even the Master's jacket on show. Then it's burgers and hot dogs, spare ribs, chicken and pasta. USGA and LGU officials speak and the captains introduce their teams and we are presented with a poster. Sweet is fruit salad, cookies and ice-cream but we leave mid-way.

Up to Jill Thornhill's room for a team chat. Emphasis on par golf again and heads held high regardless of the situation. And no bad language on the tees with all the microphones around!

It's all starting to seem more real and suddenly the practice is almost over. There's no going back now. . . . Find out later that Jill gave us the chat two nights before the match so we didn't get the collywobbles.

Friday 27
Woken by the alarm again. My back is always stiff on these mornings when my body hasn't naturally unwound out of a proper sleep. Hit a few balls and then it's our final practice, in our foursomes pairings, but we can play as many or as few holes as we want.

Today I'm going to concentrate on the four footers. If you can hole these then you can attack your first putts or pitches. On each tee, whoever is driving has to announce to her partner the line she's aiming on.

Coming down fifteen, I start to wilt a little and, after sixteen, I've had enough. That's it. If I'm not ready now, I'll never be, I'm beginning to feel excited and can't stop grinning. Julie says she woke up nervous today for a first time. Suddenly there's only a few hours to go after all the preparation. Preparation which, for me, began not just in November, but way back on the practice ground at Deeside several years ago. . . .

At the opening ceremony, the Colonial Musketeers are to lead us up the fairway. They're actually eight to fourteen-year-olds – and they're wonderful. We file in behind Jill in height order opposite our US counterpart. The side of the hill is a mass of spectators as we watch the feet in front trying to keep in step. The US flag is half raised by the time we're in position so the anthem is playing again. Then it's our turn. The Musketeers play the National Anthem and the ten of us attempt to sing. What a wonderful feeling to watch the flag being raised.

Then the various speeches about the spirit and 'friendly rivalry' of the match. It is such an honour to be a part of it. A cold shiver of anticipation runs down my back. As Mary Anderson [1991 LGU Chairman] says, no one can take this away from you. Until you're there experiencing it, no one can understand the feeling.

The foursomes are read out for tomorrow – 1. Lambert and Dobson versus Goetz and Sander; 2. Hall and Imrie versus Noble and Platt; 3. Wadsworth and Farquharson versus Semple Thompson and Weiss. It's the three Scots who are teeing off first. We later joke that it takes a Scot to handle this sort of pressure!

Saturday 28
Hear the shower next door and wake with a start. Have I slept in? No. It's only 5.17 and my alarm is set for 5.45.

Arrive at the club at 6.50 and weigh in. Then off to practise. Hit a few eight-irons followed by five-irons. Then drives. Going OK.

Move to the putting green before darting back to the clubhouse. My third visit to the loo.

Back to the first tee to see the first ones off. Catriona looks as laid back as usual, but goes all of a quiver after hitting a booming drive. Back to the range and hit a few seven-irons. Kathryn's there 'unnerving' herself by hitting more drives. She keeps going to the tee to watch and then running back to the range to hit 'just one more'.

It's my turn on the tee. My tummy is going round and round, my arms and legs are like jelly and my heart is pounding. Apart from all of that, I feel fine. I swing really slowly on my practice swing, just as I did in the Scottish. Here goes! Hit it down the middle.

At the first, they pitch to twelve feet and I knock it to six feet. They hole, we miss. 1 down.

. . . Lose at seventeenth to another American birdie.

Trail 1 to 2 at lunch. Jill stresses the importance of being out in 37 and back in 35 in the afternoon. Such scoring, she says, will win matches.

My opponent is Brandie Burton, a former international swimmer and a catcher in the realm of baseball. I lose 3 and 1 although I feel I played quite well. With Julie and Vicki winning, we finish the day trailing 3 to 6.

Jill points to how, in the foursomes, we were as many as twenty-one over par. We all know what has to be done. If we win three foursomes tomorrow, it will be neck and neck.

Sunday 29

It's hot today.

The first and second foursome pairs swop round but to no avail. Catriona and Helen Dobson win the only point on the last. Helen Wadsworth and I lose 10, 11, 12, 13 and 14 to lose 5 and 4. Not a happy game.

Playing fifth in singles against Robin Weiss. Lose first to a birdie. That's OK – game plan is to make pars. Halve second; bunkered at third: two down.

At fourth she hits green but is fifteen to twenty yards left. I knock it to six feet. She rakes her putt in and now mine has grown twenty feet. I make it – half in birdies. Halve next in par. Lose sixth to another birdie. Three down without even trying. . . .

My singles and all the others slip away, leaving us with a sorry tally of four points to the Americans' fourteen. We feel down, very down, and totally drained. All that work and we've seen it evaporate in two very short days.

Not that we can linger on our misfortune. . . .

We hurry to prepare for the closing dinner where we are seated in the middle of the marquee; US and GB alternately.

Eventually this year's captains speak and each team member is given a present from Great Britain and Ireland or the US as appropriate. There is a slide show from Curtis Cup matches past and present. The backing music is 'That's what friends are for'. . . . It will serve as a lasting memory of the occasion as it echoes everything the match represents.

Epilogue

Suddenly it's time to go home again and face the music. Many unkind and untrue comments have been stated in the media. It seems that no one likes a loser. One particular comment upsets me. 'Why did Elaine Farquharson play all four games?'

It makes me resolve to bounce back and show 'em.

It is November now and the final highlight of the season is dawning. The 1988 and 1990 Curtis Cup teams, together with the Walker and Ryder Cup sides, are invited to Buckingham Palace for a reception with the Queen and the Duke of Edinburgh.

The red carpet is out and we file up the steps to the Palace. Words cannot adequately describe the feelings we experience as we gaze in awe. It must be like living in a museum.

At around 6.10 the Queen and Prince Philip enter unannounced. We are standing in our teams in a horseshoe and one goes down one side and vice versa. Everyone is personally introduced to both the Queen and the Duke by their respective captain. We execute rather wobbly curtseys to HRH as we shake her hand. Both she and her husband ask similar questions. . . . Where do you come from? How long have you been playing golf? Do you do anything else?

Then they make general comments about golf and move on. It must be quite tedious for them as we are told they have at least two of these receptions each week plus daily audiences. Today was also the Opening of Parliament.

Approximately one hour later they depart, again unannounced. We are allowed to stay only slightly longer before being pushed gently towards the door. We emerge with our memories of 1990 all the more precious for this royal seal of approval.

CHAPTER THIRTEEN

Frances Smith

PAUSE FOR THOUGHT
BY ENID WILSON

Beginners are constantly implored to swing the club back slowly, to pause at the top before starting down, and to look at the ball.

Few of them ever manage to do as they are told, for the instincts to hurry down, and then see where the ball has gone, are impulses that golfers are always striving to bring under control.

One who demonstrates the pause at the top to a remarkable degree is Mrs Frances Smith, née Stephens. So highly developed is her control over the club that when she reaches the furthermost extent of her backswing, not only does she pause, but she stops long enough for every spectator to observe and appreciate the club is motionless.

With every club, from driver to putter, the full stop is evident at the conclusion of the backswing. Another mannerism of Mrs Smith's is her habit of taking a practice swing before every shot. Unlike most people, she performs this drill as seriously as she does the ensuing stroke.

Genius is defined as an infinite capacity for taking pains and this is an apt description of Mrs Smith's attitude towards golf.

She had the advantage of growing up with the game and was coached by her father, Fred Stephens, who was professional at the Bootle Golf Club, Liverpool.

Through constant practice, Mrs Smith has built up exceptional strength in her hands and fingers. Therein lies the secret of her control over the club and the consistency with which she keeps to the centre of the course.

The exceptional precision of Mrs Smith's game was shown in the first round of the final of the English Women's championship at Woodhall Spa in 1954, when she played the outward nine holes – length 3,200 yards – in the astounding score of thirty against the women's par of 39. Her figures included a one at the fifth.

Day in, day out, she is the best putter in British women's golf. Throughout the stroke she keeps the blade of the putter square to the

Bunty Smith, head down

intended line and, after making contact with the ball, waits to hear it drop into the hole before looking up.

In international matches for Britain and England she has won more games than any other player during the period from 1947 to 1960.

FROM *A Gallery of Women Golfers*, 1961

The late Jean Anderson and Bunty Smith, both great players in the 1940s and 1950s. Mrs Anderson, née Donald, won three Scottish Championships, while Mrs Smith, née Stephens, won three English and two British Championships

After the 1958 Curtis Cup, wherein Frances Smith defeated Polly Riley to enable Great Britain and Ireland to tie, Herb Warren Wind had no compunction in picking out this double British champion – 1949 and 1952 – for a special mention: 'She holds on to her timing in the most nerve-wracking situations because she has superb concentration. She holds on to her concentration because she has a purposefulness that never wavers and a wondrous heart.'

Much was made of the way in which 'Bunty' was not included in the 1948 Curtis Cup at Royal Birkdale, the suggestion being that the selectors of the day had been reluctant to take on board the daughter of a club professional. When it came to the next match, the then seventy-year-old Gladys Ravenscroft, who in her golfing prime had won the amateur championships of both Britain and America, took it upon herself to organise a petition on behalf of the young Lancashire golfer. Bunty was duly given a place in the 1950 side.

Whatever the rights and wrongs of what happened in connection with the 1948 match, there were never any hard feelings on Bunty's part. When her own golfing day was done, this unassuming competitor was a non-playing captain of the Great Britain and Ireland Curtis Cup side in 1962 and 1972.

Bunty, who was only fifty-three when she died in 1978, was awarded the OBE for her services to the game. A fitting tribute for a player whose pause at the top of her swing, although it was never something she did deliberately, was maybe simply another manifestation of the way in which she always thought before she spoke, said nothing rash.

Nowhere was this more appreciated than in her work as a selector. She was thorough, she was sensitive. And no one ever suspected her of picking a player for other than the right reasons.

CHAPTER FOURTEEN

Marley

Looking back over her career, Marley Harris, formerly Spearman, always saw an early altercation with the ladies at Surbiton as the occurrence which did most to ignite her golfing ambitions.

Marley had just returned cards of 103, 102 and 101 in that order to give herself a first handicap of thirty-one when she was approached by a senior member of the club. 'How would you like to play in the captain's prize? It's a stableford. . . .'

'I'd love to play,' returned Marley, 'only I don't know what a stableford is.'

'Never mind,' said the other. 'You just think of it in terms of a medal round and we'll work out your points at the end.'

Marley set forth with another novice and, as requested, the two duly handed in their cards to have them translated from medal to stableford.

As Marley's card was worked out and the mathematician in question arrived at a tally of fifty-eight points, all hell was let loose.

'*Fifty-eight points.*' The figure, recited in ever more disbelieving tones, echoed round the clubhouse.

Marley, whose initial reaction had been one of, 'Well, is that good or bad?', did not take long to appreciate that her sister members were putting it about that this was no beginner, that they had a fraud in their midst. She was summoned to have a word first with one club official, then another. Then, as she lapsed into tears in the car park, she looked back longingly to days in the theatre when everyone was so friendly and 'called you darling even if they didn't mean it . . .'.

She never was awarded that stableford prize but, on arriving home that night, received a stern lecture from her first husband, Tony Spearman, to the effect that she should either 'get out, or get down to it'.

As everyone knows, she chose the latter course and, to this day, insists that she owes everything to that slight contretemps: 'Being shot down in such a way did me nothing but good.'

Fulfilling an ambition which had been with her since her earliest years, Marley left Wimbledon High School to go on the stage as a dancer. She worked at such theatres as the Colosseum and the Adelphi but never, as was so often written in her golfing heyday, at the Windmill. There was no golf in her family and the nearest she came to having any contact with the game during her dancing years was in a golf routine in a show called *The Love Racket*. It took in the hitting of a series of imaginary golf balls and, even now, she can give a dashing resumé of the steps.

Marley's introduction to 'the real thing' has long passed into golfing lore. . . . It was a cold, wet day and, as Marley emerged from Harrods after an afternoon's shopping, there was not a cab in sight. She retreated into the store and her eyes lit on a notice reading 'Golf School'. She followed the relevant arrows.

The professional, Mr White, was in residence.

'Could I have a lesson?' asked Marley, impulsively.

'Why yes,' replied White. 'When would you like to come?'

'What's wrong with now?' hazarded Marley.

White looked long and hard at this prospective pupil. She had on high heels and a large and fashionable hat bedecked with ribbons. Marley broke the silence. 'Don't worry,' said she, with inadvertent ambiguity, 'everything comes off.'

She started hitting balls and, as was to happen so often over the ensuing months, her companion's reaction was one of sheer disbelief. 'Fantastic,' he cried. 'But of course, you've played before . . .'

Marley arrived home to find her husband and his friends discussing the game of golf they had planned for the morrow. 'Do you mind if I come?' she asked, before going on to explain how she had learnt to play in Harrods.

Carefully the men succeeded in persuading her not to join them and suggested that she should go instead to Edward Holdright's golf academy in Regent's Park.

Marley winces, still, at the memory of how she went straight up to Holdright and said, 'I'd like to use your nets.'

Holdright had always maintained that the finest swings he had ever seen came from a row of dancers in a routine such as the one in which Marley had been involved and now he watched, intrigued, as his new client hit away her quota of balls. He was mighty impressed but invited her inside on the grounds that he felt he could give her one or two useful pointers.

He spoke of theories which she could not fully absorb at that stage before closing with a statement to the effect that Marley, if she so wished, could be an international within three years. So Marley signed on for thirteen lessons from Holdright – but she was still only three weeks into the course when she had that oft-quoted round at Addington Palace.

Her husband was due to play in a four and she had accompanied him to the course with a view to having a knock on her own in some quiet

Marley Harris, who said that she had never used her hands to hold anything heavier than a tea-pot before she turned to golf, raising aloft the British trophy she won at Birkdale in 1962

corner. When one of the party failed to turn up, Marley suggested, winningly, that she take his place. Much embarrassed, Tony took her on one side. 'If you miss the ball,' he growled, 'pick it up and run.'

Marley found the whole thing a little baffling. Where she did what seemed to be the obvious thing and hit the ball straight up the middle, the other three would approach the green via the right and left rough, even bunkers: 'I couldn't understand why they were making life so difficult for themselves.'

She herself opened with a four and, so well did she continue to score that one of the men started to jot down her figures on a piece of paper out of a cigarette packet. The final total was 81 – and it was on the strength of this astonishing feat that she set about getting into the Sudbury Club.

In the aftermath of that never-to-be-forgotten captain's day, Marley settled down to a rigorous daily practice routine in her bid 'to show 'em'.

Though most of the members were still dispatching disapproving glances in her direction, there was one Mrs Doris Richards who was prepared to go against the tide. She adopted Marley, taking her to open meetings and putting her name forward for the county.

Marley needed new incentives and open meetings gave her experience of playing under pressure and on new courses. More often than not she would win – and she can remember thinking how marvellous it was that, on top of all the fun she was getting out of playing, she was accumulating a store of wonderful prizes.

Down to a handicap of four in two years, Marley was persuaded to enter her first English championship, an experience she will remember most for her opening tee shot. She had gone down to Westward Ho! a week early and enlisted the caddying services of a two-handicap golfer, a plumber by name of Harry. For seven days she practised round the course and each day she got steadily worse. 'I can remember Harry saying, "Never mind, you're going to be good one day", and my replying, "That's no use, I want to be good now".'

In the first round Marley drew Margaret Price. Mrs Price was a useful enough county golfer but, to Marley, 'she could have been Babe Zaharias herself'.

As their starting time grew close, Marley was conscious of a sea of tweed skirts gathering about the tee. A ditch crosses the first hole at Westward Ho! and, for three days, Marley had failed to make it with her shot. 'Please God,' she asked, 'let me get over this ditch today.' The ensuing swing, she felt, was heaven sent – and she looked up in time to see the ball sailing into the far distance; a glorious blow. What she could not do was pick up the tee: 'I was hopelessly in the grip of nerves, shaking all over.'

Eventually she lost the match by two and one but, for all that, the experience had been far from discouraging. Under pressure and with the adrenalin flowing, she had been able to produce some of the most telling golf of her life. True, she had messed around on the greens but, even then, there had been no question of fright. If anything, she had been over-exuberant.

Even before she made her mark in Middlesex county golf, Marley, together with another member of Sudbury in the person of John Atkins, reached the final of the Worplesdon foursomes, losing by only one hole to a partnership featuring Jacqueline Gordon of Curtis Cup fame. One noted golf writer of the day, who would later tell the story against himself, mentioned that week that Marley would never get anywhere with so long a swing.

In truth, her swing was long but, the more she practised, the firmer it became. Though many felt that the emphasis she placed on good hands owed something to the teachings of Henry Cotton, she actually worked it out for herself. 'As the hands are the things which link one to the club it was obvious to me that they had to be strong. My legs may have been in good shape from dancing but my hands were weak. Up until then I had never lifted anything heavier than a teapot.'

In 1954, Marley won the Scratch medal in the Middlesex county championship as a prelude to winning the championship itself in each of the next five years. In all, she was to win it eight times.

It was in 1955, when she was asked to play for England in the Home Internationals at Royal Portrush, that Marley suddenly became conscious of a change in outlook. Having always found the game absurdly easy, she suddenly became aware of the pitfalls, an experience she has since likened to 'going into a dark tunnel'.

With the prospect of playing for her country looming, she felt a certain sense of responsibility – and so began a gruelling period in which, in the garage below the mews flat where she lived, she would practice till all hours. She was driven by the same desire that she had had in the years on stage to give a perfect performance on the day but, at the same time, she loved the hard work: 'Practice, with all its intrinsic disciplines, is a wonderful part of the sport. You can give yourself so much more than just a good game of golf.'

Marley has always believed that the swing you are born with is the swing you die with. She herself had an upright swing and set to work on making it repeat. She cites Lee Trevino as a player who is faithful to his own swing plane. 'He hits everything in a banana – but he knows his banana, allows for it. That is the shape of shot he will always hit under pressure and, at least to my mind, it makes sense to hit it that way all the time.'

Marley eventually reached a stage where she could tell, by feel, whether she was shut or open at the top of her swing, she was always very much more conscious of what happened in the hitting area 'where so many tend to pack up'.

By then she was doing more work on her hands – hitting against a rolled-up carpet and lifting weights. This did much, she felt, to help her find the ball and stay behind it. However, much though she would stress the importance of the hands, she concentrated, above all, on a flowing swing.

Practice apart, Marley reckoned that the amount of golf she had played with men had had much to do with her making it to international level. So used was she to playing off men's tees and doing things at their most difficult that, when it came to playing a course set up for a women's event, everything seemed easy. Similarly, she got used to being outdriven – something which meant that, on those rare occasions when she was out-hit by someone of her own sex, she was not unduly disturbed: 'Because I had so often hit my second shots first, I reached a stage where my fairway woods became as sharp as my middle or even short irons.'

With men generally being regarded as superior beings on the golf front, Marley felt that a desire not to make a fool of herself in their company further contributed to her advance: 'If I made a mistake, I made darned sure that I made up for it with a good chip, putt or whatever . . .'

Marley played for England for eleven successive years from 1955, while she represented Great Britain in the Curtis Cup in each of 1960, 1962 and 1964. In the 1964 match at Royal Porthcawl, she gave the home side an inspired lead by winning both foursomes with Angela Bonallack and halving her singles against Barbara McIntire and Jo-Anne Carner.

The halved game against the latter is a match she nominates as one of the three best of her career. The other two were her semi-final victory over Brigitte Varangot in the British championship she won at Carnoustie and the match in which she beat Angela Bonallack to reach the final of the English at Lytham.

Against Brigitte, Marley was taken to the twenty-third in a game which caught the imagination of half the town. Both were short of the green in two at Carnoustie's fifth or twenty-third hole – and it was the French girl to play first. Judging her little chip-and-run to perfection, she ran her ball up to within a couple of inches of the hole.

Marley, as was frequently her wont in such situations, prayed that she might be allowed to get if not inside Brigitte's ball, then at least the same distance away. Whereupon she hit her little chip – as far as she can recall with an eight-iron – straight into the cup to clinch the match.

Her game at Lytham with Angela was another extra-time affair and one which she remembers as being played in a marvellous spirit: 'I was lucky to play in the time of Angela. I liked her enormously. She was a terrific golfer and I had the utmost admiration for her tenacity.' Such sentiments were echoed by JoAnne Carner when the American was giving her views on the best British competitors of her Curtis Cup years.

Marley herself was an instinctively good sport who, away from the jealousy on the part of others in her early days, endeared herself to everyone. She was always considerate and quick to acknowledge a good shot.

Partly because of her stage career and partly because she always had the confidence of one who knew she had done her homework to the best of her ability, she had about her a certain aura. There were those who, when drawn against her, would feel a couple of holes to the bad before ever they left the first tee – but there were others for whom a match against Marley was something of an inspiration.

Marley loved a good competitor and was always more than a little irritated when it was said of someone that they were 'too nice to win'. To Marley, a player thus categorised was simply lacking in guts.

Not that she herself did not know how easy it was to slip into thinking badly. . . .In the British she was destined to win at Birkdale, there was one occasion when she inadvertently tuned into a conversation behind the next row of lockers as she was preparing to play an early round. A gathering of women golfers were exhorting their friend along the lines, 'Marley won't know what's hit her when you start putting'.

The woman in question had not a clue where the long game was concerned, often taking twice as many shots as Marley to reach the green. Once on the putting surface, though, she was every inch the demon her supporters had been making out. Time after time she would get down in one putt, leaving a disconcerted and disorientated Marley thinking along the lines, 'I've only got to take three putts for the half'.

The woman's husband was in evidence, talking enthusiastically to Marley about his wife's prowess on the greens and, when it came to the turn, Marley was one down.

A cluster of golf writers including Pat Ward Thomas of *The Guardian* and Peter Ryde of *The Times* had popped up at the back of the ninth green to check on the state of the match – and their reaction to the news that Marley was down was such that their heroine was stung back to life: 'I just managed in time to cut myself off from the husband and wife, concentrate on my own golf.'

Another case of her thinking being less than positive came when she was representing Great Britain and Ireland for the first time in the Vagliano Trophy match. In what was a thirty-six hole singles, Marley had gone into lunch ten up but, when play resumed in the afternoon, had lost the first hole. 'Heavens!' she cried to her caddie, 'I'm only nine up.'

For the most part, Marley's experiences in team golf mostly conjured up good memories. She loved the company of her international contemporaries – 'they were all masses of fun' – but she particularly likes to look back on earlier days in the Middlesex county team. 'Middlesex were a wonderful side. We barely had enough players to make up a first team, but we were always laughing, always trying our hearts out. I would have to say that those county matches represented some of my best times in golf.'

Marley never felt that time spent working on an amateur game was wasted. She herself never had any desire to turn professional and one had the impression that she felt it all too easy for a woman turning professional to get her priorities wrong.

One player she has always cited as having survived the pressure of women's professional golf in the States is Nancy Lopez. . . . 'Nancy stands out like a diamond on the LPGA tour. She is alive, vibrant and clearly sees golf for what it is – nothing more than a game.'

Marley's outlook was one which, on the birth of her son, Mark, had her stepping out of the competitive arena without a second thought. 'Mind you,' she said, 'I don't think there is anything to be gained from hanging on. It may be wrong, but I would have hated to have got to the stage where I was simply making up the numbers. Right through my career, I knew I wanted to get out at a time when I was winning.'

No one doubts that her view on such matters was coloured by what happened to Judy Garland. The film star was Marley's great heroine until that day Marley went to see her at the Palladium at a time when she had become almost a caricature of her former self. 'It was,' said Marley, 'one of the saddest things I have seen in my life. What a pity she hadn't stopped, left us with lovely memories of how she was at her best.'

When Bridget Jackson was recently asked by *The Edgbastonian* what she would take with her to a desert island, the 1956 English champion and Curtis Cup golfer opted for 'a suitcase full of scrap books, which would help revive memories of four decades of playing and being connected with the amateur side of the Royal and Ancient Game of Golf.'

In an excerpt from her article, the Birmingham golfer tells of a team trip Down Under – one of the last such golfing expeditions to be made by sea:

'In 1951 my father entered me for the British Girls' championship at Gullane. What an eye-opener this proved to be. Seeing older girls producing first-class golf in contrast to my high-handicap efforts. Ambition was kindled and when I returned to Scotland three years later, I succeeded in winning the championship.

This success proved to be a stepping stone to being selected for a seven-month tour to Australia and New Zealand with four other juniors [including Veronica Beharrell – née Anstey from Edgbaston] and a senior captain.

After sailing out of Tilbury on the *Orantes* and having the usual rough crossing of the Bay of Biscay, my recollections are of seeing Gibraltar at daybreak; Naples, where, taking a taxi, we saw much of the city and visited a cameo factory; Port Said, with the sights and smells of a busy Middle Eastern port; the marvels of the Suez Canal; the heat of Aden where we encountered many street hawkers; then across the Arabian Sea to Ceylon [Sri Lanka]. After anchoring off Colombo, members of the Royal Colombo Golf Club took us off by launch and car for a memorable match against the club and a marvellous luncheon party at the Colombo Club. Then, twelve hours later, back on board for the voyage across the Indian Ocean to Freemantle. The drive along the banks of the Swan River, in brilliant sunshine, was a great introduction to Perth and Australia.

During our three-month tour of Australia we travelled nearly ten thousand miles by air. We visited all the states, spending a week in each of Western and South Australia and Tasmania; eighteen days in Victoria; three weeks in Queensland; and six in New South Wales.

Although I remember the golf on many interesting and exciting courses, other memories are of visiting sheep stations, the Great Barrier Reef, a boat trip round Sydney Harbour, my birthday celebration at a winery, a match in the Victorian championship against Joan Hammond of operatic fame, and visiting Canberra to see Parliament House and the War Memorial and Museum.

Thereafter there was a flight over the Tasman Sea to New Zealand for seven weeks, four of which were spent in the North Island. Much of our travelling was by car which gave us the opportunity to see the countryside. Apart from the golf, there were visits to the Wellington Races, the Naval Trafalgar Day Ball at Nelson, a tour of a butter and cheese-making factory and our Test Match against the Maoris. None of us will forget the welcoming haka and the feast and entertainment in one of their meeting houses. And after this the visit to the thermal region in and around Rotorua.

Finally, a return voyage home from Wellington to Southampton via Panama and Curaçao. The relaxing time on board the *Rangitiki* gave us the chance to reflect on the great loyalty shown to the Queen; and on the generous hospitality and·many kindnesses and mementos received.

What an experience for a nineteen-year-old!'

The Rawlings, then and now

CHAPTER FIFTEEN

Wales's First Family

With 1986 a Curtis Cup year, officials of the United States Golf Association were sitting round a table at Golf House, New Jersey, to discuss their shortlist for the American team. To the names of those who had shone in 1985 had been added some among the best-placed competitors from the Orange Blossom circuit held at the start of 1986 in Florida.

'This Vicki Thomas,' ventured one of the USGA ladies, perusing the Florida results, 'looks exactly the kind of player we need.'

'Well,' came the mischievously sensational reply from across the table, 'you can't have her!'

There was then a pause before the lady in question went on to explain to her bemused audience that 'this Vicki Thomas' was Welsh rather than American and that she would be teeing up for the opposition.

Vicki, who was born in 1954 and has to date played in five Curtis Cups and four Commonwealth tournaments, is the oldest of Granville and Joyce Rawlings's three golfing daughters. Where she has won six Welsh titles and Mandy, her youngest sister, has won that championship twice, all three of Vicki, Mandy and Kerry have their names on the Welsh junior championship trophy. Again, all three represented their country in the Home Internationals of 1979.

Yet, despite their achievements, these engagingly garrulous Welsh golfers have no hesitation in naming their mother as the real success story. . . .

Vicki was leaving the British championship at Conwy in 1981 when she learned how her mother, who was suffering from leukaemia, had been given less than a year to live.

An eleven handicap golfer when illness struck, Joyce lost her handicap as she fought for her life. However, with Kerry producing her first grandaughter, and Vicki and Mandy bombarding her with one tournament win after another, she picked up in a way which was the antithesis of the golfing sense.

It was in 1986 that the medical men finally confirmed that the leukaemia was under control. Vicki celebrated at once by writing away to the LGU to establish how – and at what point – her mother could get back on the handicap ladder. The answer was that she should re-start at eighteen – and this she did, wasting no time in lopping a couple of shots off that figure.

Like the rest of the family, Joyce has had the benefit of a teacher, Granville, who has what Vicki calls 'a natural aptitude' for seeing faults. Where Vicki is concerned, Mr Rawlings stresses nothing so much as that she should concentrate on rhythm and timing, while the favourite image he has given her over the years is one of starting the club back close to the ground 'like an aeroplane preparing for take-off'.

Having been introduced to golf by his boss, Mr Rawlings took the game home to his family and it duly became one of those areas in which he would stand for no nonense from his young daughters, expecting them to rise at weekends for early morning practice sessions.

At an hour when other Welsh children would be filing off to chapel on a Sunday morning, the Rawlings trio would be lining up on the practice ground. Mr Rawlings's creed, explained Vicki, with a twinkle, was one to the effect that practice shots brought their own salvation.

The girls reacted in different ways to this regime. Vicki, who throughout her teenage years found ball-games rather more irresistible than boys, went along uncomplainingly with her father's wishes. Kerry and Mandy, for their part, felt ill-disposed towards these early-morning starts – especially when they followed late-night discos. 'Come off it, Dad,' they would protest as the alarm rang. Occasionally, their cry would be echoed by their mother but, as Vicki remembers it, Mrs Rawlings mostly avoided getting involved.

Mr Rawlings persevered in trying to get across to the two younger ones that there was time only for golf and schoolwork if they were to do both well, but they demanded – and achieved – the odd compromise.

Yet, even if Kerry and Mandy were not quite as committed as he would have wished, all three were chosen to represent their country in the aforementioned Home Internationals of 1979, the year in which they had earlier played alongside their mother in the five-strong Bargoed team which won the Welsh Club championship.

In running through the strengths each sister brought to bear, Vicki reckons that she was always the most rounded golfer of the trio. Mandy, who was at one stage down to scratch, hit the ball far and well, and Kerry, who played to four, excelled with the little shots on and around the green. 'Kerry was almost a Faldo when it came to putting', remembers Vicki. 'She seldom three-putted and holed an enormous number of fifteen-footers. It wasn't just luck. She did it far too often for that . . .'

Those Home Internationals at Harlech were in every sense memorable. Kerry, three months pregnant at the time, defeated no less a player than Ita Butler to give Wales a win over Ireland. That, in turn, enabled Scotland to win the championship, with England finishing last. To this day, Vicki can still see the crowds swarming down the eighteenth. . . .

Because it was in Scotland's interests that Wales should win and England's interests that the Irish should prevail, the Welsh and the Scottish players and supporters walked down one side of the fairway, with the English and Irish down the other. 'When Kerry won,' recalls Vicki, wincing still at the memory, 'the Scots threw her in the air.'

Not that it did her any harm. In March 1980 she gave birth to the grandchild who was to be so great a source of inspiration to Joyce Rawlings. Whereas, from that point, the middle sister was restricted to club and county golf, Mandy was showing signs of fulfilling her great golfing potential. At fifteen, she won the first of two successive Welsh championships; at sixteen she was chosen to play for Great Britain and Ireland in the Vagliano Trophy match.

In common with so many who hit the heights at an early age, there was then a lull before she enjoyed the distinction of being unbeaten in the Home Internationals of 1986. Mind you, she had by then acquired what her father must have seen as the ideal suitor. Namely, an assistant professional by name of Gary Illingworth who is today the professional at Heidelberg. They are now married, with Gary having carried on Mr Rawlings's good work in keeping Mandy, an often easily distracted soul, at her golf. Fluent in Welsh as the result of being the only one of the three to attend a Welsh-speaking school, Mandy had no trouble adjusting to German and, indeed, was fluent in that language in a matter of months.

And what of Vicki? After attending PE college, she won the Welsh championship of 1979 and was runner-up in the British Women's Stroke-Play championship of that year before taking on a full-time job and a husband, Graham Thomas. As you will have guessed, she met Graham, a General Accident inspector, through golf, with the occasion in question a match between the Pennard men and the Glamorgan Ladies' county side.

There came a day, as she sank into a chair at the end of the long drive from her job in Caerphilly, forty miles from their home in Bishopston, that Vicki said to Graham, 'This is killing me.'

With no teaching jobs to be had nearer home, his suggestion was that she should call it a day and play some golf. Thanks to her father's training, Vicki did not find it difficult to get back in the habit of practising. It helped, too, that she was able to play with her husband and his friends at Pennard, and that Graham offered nothing but encouragement.

There was encouragement, too, from Welsh officialdom. Vicki, who today does all she can to help up-and-coming Welsh golfers, marvels at the quietly efficient way in which the women of the Welsh Ladies' Golf Union go about their business. She will, she says, never forget the day she learned that Pat Roberts, secretary of the Union, had rather more on her curriculum vitae than merely secretarial skills. 'I went to Newport Golf Club one morning and there it was up on the board,' she recalls. 'Pat Roberts had been the Welsh champion three times; the runner-up seven times; a member of the World Cup side of 1964; and a regular member of the Welsh side for the Home Internationals from 1950 to 1970. Closer to home, she had won no fewer than eighteen Monmouthshire County titles and twenty-five Newport club championships. A terrific record.'

Welsh champion for a second time in 1982, Vicki never looked back. She was chosen for the Curtis Cup side of that year and, of course, has never been out of the team since. From the two occasions Great Britain and Ireland won – in 1986 and 1988 – she gleaned three and a half out of a possible five points, that tally taking in two singles wins.

As a team member, she is second to none, although her sportingly selfless approach can sometimes work against her. If, for instance, a captain were to ask herself who would react best to being dropped from a particular series of matches, she would doubtless hit on Vicki. What is more, that captain could rest assured that the Welsh player would spend the afternoon encouraging the others rather than feeling sorry for herself.

On the course, Vicki benefits from the same, make-the-best-of-everything approach. Long and straight off the tee and endlessly reliable with the middle irons, she acknowledges that she is not as good as she might be when the occasion demands a half or three-quarter wedge. Without being obsessive, she practises the shot religiously.

This Welsh golfing heroine will usually do one of two things when her game is below its best. If she is at home, she will go and see Michael Bennett, the professional who has kept an eye on so many of her practice hours at Pennard. If she is in the vicinity of Wentworth, she will call Bernard Gallacher, who is so much in tune with the Curtis Cup squad.

The Ryder Cup captain says that the older Vicki gets, the more impressive she becomes. 'She is a wonderfully dependable and determined golfer, but what I like best about her is the fact she knows her own game well. Most women are apt to sit back when they have a professional and depend on him too heavily. Myself, I always teach people to try to be independent and Vicki scores well in this department.'

Tickled though she might be at Bernard's assessment, Vicki concedes that there are still occasions when she feels the need to call her father who, she says, 'will always know me and my game better than I do myself'.

Though she achieved a lifetime's ambition when she won her first British championship in 1990, the Stroke-Play at Strathaven, Vicki says that her most poignant moment came some weeks earlier when she was playing in front of her family in the Curtis Cup at Somerset Hills. Joyce Rawlings dislikes flying but agreed to make the trip when Vicki hoodwinked her into believing that the flight from Heathrow to Newark was 'just a couple of hours'. Only when they were airborne did she admit that it would maybe take a little longer.

The match had got off to a bad start from the visitors' point of view and Great Britain and Ireland were in grave danger of slipping to a 2 to 7 deficit on the first day. No one was holding out any hope of an improvement on that tally when suddenly Vicki came back from one down with two to play to beat that bastion of American amateur golf, Carol Semple Thompson, on the eighteenth green.

It made the score 3 to 6 and it made her husband and her mother, not to mention the father who taught her, inordinately proud.

Liz Chadwick, now Pook. British Champion in 1966 and 1967 Inset: Liz Chadwick and Catherine Lacoste after their epic battle at Ganton in 1966, when the Cheshire girl holed a 35-foot putt to win on the 20th. 'Catherine was one of the first to contact me after my accident, which was wonderful for my morale,' said Liz

CHAPTER SIXTEEN

When Pain is Par

When Joanne Morley won the 1991 *Daily Telegraph*'s Woman Golfer of the Year Award, she spoke at the presentation about the help she had received from others. Her mother, Jean, was one among those she picked out, and she also made mention of Liz Pook, a sister member of Cheshire and the winner of the British Women's championship in each of 1966 and 1967.

In overcoming a handful of disappointments while playing her way to the top of the British amateur game, Joanne had time and time again been cheered by notes of encouragement from Liz Pook. The notes were more than usually inspiring, for Joanne knew, only too well, that her sufferings were as nothing to those of the writer. . . .

Liz Pook, née Chadwick, was one of the game's great fighters. She had twos at all the short holes before making the 35-footer which enabled her to beat the great Catherine Lacoste in the British Championship at Ganton in 1966 and she came back from four down after five holes to defeat Linda Bayman in the first round the following year.

Having left the tournament circuit in order to start a family, Liz was in 1986 on the point of returning to golf – she even toyed with the notion of becoming a teaching professional – when an operation on her back went badly wrong.

The accident which left this most plucky of champions fighting paralysis rather than par had its origins in a game of tennis. Captain of the B team at Buckden, the village where she and her husband, Tony, lived at that time with their two children, Andrew and Caroline, the former Curtis Cup golfer had been despairing that her backhand was so much weaker than her forehand.

'Try a double-hander,' someone had suggested, helpfully. She did, but succeeded only in slipping a disc. With the pain shifting, rather than subsiding, she was subjected to several tests until, in January 1987, she was told by Addenbrooke's Hospital that one test had revealed a tumour in the thorax area which needed immediate attention.

With one thing or another – most notably an inflammation under her left arm which refused to settle – surgery had to be delayed until April. But by then she was organised, apart from anything else, having prepared the eighty-eight frozen meals needed to tide her family over the three weeks she expected to be in hospital.

When the operation finally went ahead, whatever it was they had seen on the scan – probably a blood clot – had disappeared. But her spine was in a state of shock from the exploratory surgery. She was paralysed from the waist down and unable to write properly.

Her faith stopped her from feeling angry. A committed Christian who had never allowed her golfing travels to interfere with church-going, Liz drew strength from talking to patients worse off than herself.

There was an occasion, though, when she let fly. With her emotions disturbed by all the drugs she was having to take, she took aim on a psychiatrist with a glass of water. It was an action which, she added, with customary humour, may have explained the way in which the psychiatrist at Stoke Mandeville gingerly introduced himself when she arrived there in June of that year.

Taught to make adventurous use of her wheelchair by the two war-savaged Lebanese boys brought to Stoke Mandeville by Dr Pauline Cutting, Liz surprised all those who had doubted that she would ever walk again and was released shortly before Christmas.

For a long time, a thick paperback book, *The Disabled Rights Handbook*, was as handy as any dictionary or cookery book. 'Worse than *The Rules of Golf*,' she would protest, laughingly.

Help has come from many quarters. . . . After an appeal from the former county captain and current president of the LGU, Carol Comboy, Cheshire provided a light-weight wheelchair and the special hand controls needed to adapt her car. More recently, to cite another example, the members of her club, Bramall Park, gave her a computer which, she says, 'has opened a whole new world for me'.

By way of a hobby, she and her husband collect old golf books. Their collection on women's golf is extensive and Liz was able to give much help with this LGU Centenary book. And if that were not enough, she keeps in touch with many of the 2,000 people who have written to her since that fateful day when the operation on her back went so wrong.

To this day, her legs have felt all the time as if in a vice but, by wearing a caliper on her right leg and using two sticks, she can move slowly about the family home near Bath. She has accepted invitations to attend tournaments, and she has also forced herself to give many a talk with a view to boosting funds for the Spinal Injuries Association. 'Why I do them,' she confided, 'is something I can't quite comprehend. . . . I get so nervous.' Those who know her well would suggest that it is merely another manifestation of the fibre she showed all her golfing days.

Of all her achievements in golf, it is her record *vis-à-vis* the aforementioned Catherine Lacoste of which she is most proud. Over the five matches they played, Liz won three, halved one and lost one; their meeting in an unofficial international with France at Royal St George's in 1966 is the one she described in a recent note as 'a real belter of a match. . . . Somehow I was out in 33 and three up, having holed out with my six-iron for an eagle two at the fifth. It was a blind second, and I can see myself now, running up the hillocks in the expectation of spotting the ball close to the flag but little thinking it would have dropped. Catherine fought back, winning two holes. Then, at the fourteenth, I holed a chip to go back to two ahead. By way of a reply, she holed chips at each of the fifteenth and sixteenth before finally we finished all square.'

By way of a brief footnote she added, 'I would sooner a match finished in that manner than win in a scrappy fashion any day.'

Rather than dwell on the things which have gone wrong, Liz has concentrated on the brighter side and, in so doing, has been a shining light to golfers everywhere who might otherwise have got things out of perspective.

She points to how, since the accident, her life has been enriched by the kindness of friends and the brave people she encountered in hospital. She gave a special mention to Jane Brittain, a former Staffordshire County player she met recently at the pain research programme. Again, she will tell you that her family, which had been close in the first place, has become still more tight-knit, with her husband the proverbial tower of strength. Her son and daughter – and this is as telling a tribute as any to the way in which she has handled her demise – have both chosen to work in the caring professions, her son with the elderly and her daughter with children.

In her golfing days, Liz swore by Vincent Peale's *Power of Positive Thinking*. Gary Player, whose card she marked in the 1967 Open, had preceded her as a disciple and, indeed, the South African autographed her copy of the book.

Now the philosophy implicit in Peale's treatise has shrunk to an inscription on a little card sent to her at Addenbrooke's when she was at her lowest. 'Misfortune,' it counselled, 'is an occasion to demonstrate character.'

Two Holes In One

'Russell staggered over Double Aces', ran the headline in the *Daily Telegraph* of Wednesday, 4 October 1989.

The event in which Wendy Russell, an LGU official, performed this extraordinary event was the British Seniors' championship, a competition for the Over-50s which has never quite added up to the sedate contest suggested by its title. In 1990, to cite a second example, Catherine Bailey, the defending champion, emerged from a welcoming party at the Harrogate Golf Club to find that her clubs and the championship trophy had disappeared, along with her car. Then, in 1991 at Ladybank, there was a last-round incident which had the LGU leafing frantically through their rule-books. The incident in question concerned Elizabeth Simpson, a member of the Murrayfield club in Edinburgh whose ball, at Ladybank's sixteenth, had come to rest on top of a dead rabbit. (This was in every sense a pretty messy affair – Mrs Simpson had to play the ball as it lay.)

Reverting to Wendy Russell's two aces, the venue was Wrexham and the timing the championship's first morning.

Ace Number 1 – at the 127-yards fourth – left her rather more than a little bashful. Though her seven-iron had sounded healthy enough, the ball rebounded off a greenside tree en route to the hole.

Diana Pritchard, the current chairman of the LGU and an excited witness to events at the fourth, caught up with Wendy anew as she was taking the tee at the 118-yards eighth.

'How's it going now?' asked Diana.

'I could do with another hole in one,' replied Wendy, in an oblique reference to the putts she had missed at the sixth and seventh.

This time she opted for a leisurely eight-iron and took aim on the right-hand bank. She watched in mingled astonishment and disbelief as her ball rolled towards the hole – and dropped confidently in its middle – for a second time. In the face of this sensational double, the player kept uncannily calm, explaining, 'It was as if it weren't happening to me.'

Then, without any help in the way of holes in one, she proceeded to come home in 39 to match her outward half. All were delighted for the Broadstone golfer, feeling that no one was more deserving of a day in the limelight. In the eight years leading up to that championship she had quietly donated £15,000 to English girls' golf as a result of the golfing

Wendy Russell receiving an award for her two holes in one on the first day of the 1989 British Women's Senior Championship at Wrexham

headcover business she had started with a view to giving work to the first of the Vietnamese boat people.

When she had come in off the course and answered the multifarious press questions, Wendy slipped away to phone her husband, a Bournemouth-based doctor who, in such circumstances, was not going to mind being dragged away from his afternoon surgery.

But Wendy, with her inadvertent ambiguity, could scarcely have made a greater hash of delivering her news of a lifetime.

'Darling,' she said, 'I've done two holes in two!'

MULTIPLE ACES

Ruth Ferguson's youthful enthusiasm maybe owes something to her regular diet of holes in one. Fourteen, at the last count.

A finalist in the English championship in 1956 and winner of the Northern in 1960, Ruth, a regular competitor in the British Senior championship, remembers her first ace as having occurred at Saddleworth: 'I hit the pin with a seven-iron and the ball went straight down the hole. . . . It was such a thrill to see it disappear.'

If that hole in one has remained a particular favourite so, too, has the one she notched as Lancashire played Northumberland. She was partnering Ann Howard of Curtis Cup fame and her ace had them winning their match by one hole.

There was a hole-in-one to spice up the mixed foursomes she won with her husband, Freddie, at Harlech; and another at Mere which contributed to her winning of the Dorothy Perkins Trophy.

She had one at the Manchester Golf Club, one at Crompton and Royton – and another at Los Monteros, 'an uphill hole where the ball hit a rock-face and amazingly was in the hole when we got there!'

Had she not mislaid the relevant list she uses to jog her memory, Ruth would no doubt have been able to call to mind the other seven. As it is, she is still too busy making golfing history to have time to dwell on past aces and places.

CHAPTER SEVENTEEN

From Mother to Daughter

As a youngster, Catherine Lacoste was wholly in the shadow of the most famous set of sporting parents France has to offer. Her father, René Lacoste, won Wimbledon in 1925 and 1928, while her mother, as Simone de la Chaume, was the first French golfer to win the British Girls' championship (1924) and, three years later, the first to win the British championship itself. Not since Lottie Dod, who was five times a Wimbledon champion before winning golf's British championship of 1904, had tennis and golf been so tellingly interwoven.

Catherine Lacoste, for her part, was uppermost on the French junior scene and went on to finish in a share of first place for the individual award at the 1964 Espirito Santo or World Team championships. But it was only when, at twenty-two, she won the 1967 American Women's Open that she felt she had emerged as a person in her own right. 'All of a sudden,' she was moved to say, 'I feel I am someone myself . . . not just the daughter of the Lacostes.'

Mlle Simone de la Chaume had been taught, as a child, by Arnaud Massey, the first overseas player to win the Open. Always to the forefront as a junior, she first came to prominence on the senior scene in the 1925 French Open at Versailles where she was runner-up to America's Glenna Collett.

The French player and the match itself were to remain clearly etched in the American's memory: 'It was a thrilling duel with Simone, then seventeen, displaying a high degree of intrepidity and skill for the first eighteen holes. That left us even, but in the following round she failed to put forward the blazing exhibition of golf that marked her initial game and I won on the thirty-fifth green.'

Miss Collett described her young opponent as 'slightly-built' before adding that she effected 'a rugged, full swing which gives her remarkable distance off the tees. Her short game is equal to the best, and added to that she has a charming personality which endears her to any gallery.'

*Mme Simone de la Chaume, winner of the 1927 British Ladies' Championship. Her
daughter, Catherine Lacoste added her name to the trophy in 1969*

In the following year Mlle de la Chaume defeated Cecil Leitch and
all the Silloth golfer's compatriots in winning the British championship at
Newcastle County Down. As was the case in the British Girls' championship she had won at Stoke Poges, her opponent in the final at Newcastle
County Down was Dorothy Pearson.

The Parisian, who would become one of the game's great stylists,
both in the way she dressed and the way she played, had just given birth
to her first child, a son, when she competed in the inaugural France–Britain
international. Joyce Wethered, a great friend and admirer of the French
player, beat her by 5 and 4 in the leading match of the afternoon but was
quick to suggest that the margin of her win owed most to her opponent's

Catherine Lacoste accepting the team award for France at the 1966 British Women's Championship at Ganton. The French won by a little matter of twenty shots

thoughts 'having occasionally drifted to Lacoste junior, whom I had the pleasure of seeing when passing through Paris in the following year'.

The LGU's newly-formed International Hospitality Committee organised a dinner at the Savoy on the night of the match for the teams and their male escorts. Jean Borotra, like René Lacoste, one of the so-called 'Three Musketeers', was among the guests, with Miss Wethered remembering his flying visit as follows: 'With his usual grace, he kissed the hands of all the lady golfers, stayed for a few dances and then very characteristically disappeared as suddenly as he had arrived.'

That Mme Lacoste's daughter was good by world standards was apparent to everyone who attended the aforementioned World Team championships of 1964. Very much the junior in a side otherwise comprising Brigitte Varangot and Claudine Cros, she played the major part in France's win; also, her achievement in sharing the individual honours with America's Carol Sorenson was nothing short of sensational for one who was still relatively unknown outside her native land.

Following this result, Catherine's visits to Britain attracted rather more in the way of attention. In the realm of medal-play, she delighted her supporters with the 66 she returned in the course of winning the 1966 Astor Salver at Prince's. In match-play, though, she for long remained vulnerable, being all too conscious of the luck which attached to this format.

Liz Pook, the British player against whom she always seemed to be drawn when playing in Britain – the Cheshire player's record against her was won three, halved one and lost one – felt that she knew how to play Catherine, though she would always add the rider that their matches together were all before the French player peaked: 'I was happy for her to knock her drives out of sight because it enabled me to get my second in first. Also, I tried not to watch her too closely, because the sight of her hitting through the ball was not something you could put to the back of your mind. It was frighteningly powerful.'

In rummaging through her collection of golfing books not so long ago, Liz Pook discovered that the swings of Catherine Lacoste and Cecil Leitch, the player Catherine's mother had defeated in that French Open of 1926, were not dissimilar – at least at the top. 'It would have been interesting,' she mused, 'to place a set of 1960s clothes on Miss Leitch – and likewise slip Catherine into a headband, tie, floppy cardigan and longish tweed skirt!'

It was in 1967 that Catherine won her first French Open championship – and from there took aim on the American Open at Hot Springs, Virginia.

This was the first time she would travel to a tournament on her own and she was revelling in her new-found independence one minute and feeling apprehensive the next. She played practice rounds with an assistant professional at the club who pointed her out to the press as a player to watch, but the extensive newspaper previews scarcely touched on the visiting French champion.

By the half-way stage, Catherine was five shots ahead of her illustrious American rivals. Ultimately, she won by two to become the youngest player to get her name on the trophy; the first foreigner to win the title; and the first amateur. Some among the American professionals had been sporting enough in the wake of this embarrassing defeat but there were others, as Catherine saw it at the time, who had seemed hell-bent on looking for reasons to disqualify her, to catch her out.

It maybe did not help her cause that she was light years removed from the kind of endearingly unassuming soul that was Laura Davies when she beat the Americans in their own back yard. Catherine radiated confidence and was often as uninhibited with her comments as she was with her one-iron, a club she used to more devastating effect than any other woman since the Babe.

Yet there was no one with a warmer heart. She was as fiercely devoted to her family and friends as she was to her golf and when, in 1969, she at last matched her mother's feat in winning the British Women's championship, she said that nothing had given her greater pleasure than that her mother was at Portrush to see it all.

Four down against Ann Irvin in the final, Catherine demonstrated the best of her fighting qualities in coming back to win on the home green. Having already that year won the Spanish and the French championships, she then decided to try for the US Amateur, the only major title in the amateur game to have eluded her.

She was engaged to be married at the time and knew that this would probably represent the last occasion she would be able to make an all-out assault on any championship. It was nothing less than an all-out assault. She clawed her way back from three down against Anne Sander in the semi-final before defeating Shelley Hamlin by three and two in another cracking game. Hers was a stupendous effort and one which left her spent and happy enough to retire.

Had it all happened ten to fifteen years later, she would doubtless have been lured into the professional life. As it is, she feels she got the maximum out of the game, playing amateur golf to the highest level before bringing up her impressively multi-lingual family of four on the edge of Madrid.

Catherine believes that she could never have become accustomed to all the travelling required in the professional game, and she was never sure that the toughness required to win championships was without its destructive side. 'I felt,' she said, 'that the effort involved whenever I won somehow cost me another piece of my sensitivity. I was becoming too hard as a person, unable to switch off once the game was over.'

Yet, to those who knew her well, she handled that combination of famous parents and her own fame decidedly well – and never without a genuine humour. There were countless Catherine Lacoste stories, such as the one of how, when the food was some way below par in a team event in Scandinavia, she called for steaks to be flown in from Paris.

Most of the stories have grown in the telling, but the one about Mr Pompidou, she laughingly revealed, was roughly true. . . .

At the start of some junior trip, when there was trouble with a couple of her team-mates' passports, Catherine took it upon herself to sort things out by the simple expedient of making a phone-call to the then French premier. (That he was an old family friend did nothing to quell the open-mouthed astonishment of those about her.)

Later that year, Catherine was the patently proud recipient of a birthday card bearing a fond inscription from Monsieur Pompidou. Her excitement, however, was short-lived. As you would have expected, her friends were unable to remain quiet on the subject of how it was they – not the French premier – who had sent the missive in question.

CHAPTER EIGHTEEN

Second Innings

Jill Thornhill and Angela Uzielli both returned to play at the highest level after they were convinced their championship days were done. Jill was a twenty-one-year-old member of the Vagliano Trophy side who did not play again in that team until she was forty-one. As for Angela, she won the British championship of 1977 before re-emerging in 1990 to win both the English Women's championship and the British Women's Senior championship.

JILL THORNHILL

Many a woman golfer's career is interrupted by child-rearing and Jill Thornhill's was no exception. She had just made the England team and the 1963 British side for the Vagliano Trophy match when her daughter, Caroline, was born; and she had just returned to the England fray when Mark came along.

The Surrey golfer was getting nicely back into her stride in the 1970s – she played in her second European Team championships in 1973 and reached the final of the 1974 English championship – when there came a third interruption. This added up to rather more than merely 'a pregnant pause', for her husband, John, was being offered a four-year contract in Saudi Arabia to work with the company managing the port of Jedda.

Jill accepted that this particular break was going to spell the end of her tournament aspirations but it never occurred to her not to go. 'People who visited us in Saudi,' she recalls, 'would ask, "How can you put up with this for so long?" but, to me, it was a great experience.'

Even if her golfing ambitions expired during that Middle Eastern sojourn, her competitive fire was kept aflicker by the friendly games she would have on the nine-hole course – all sand and no greens – on the American complex at Jedda.

Again, there was a revealing occasion when she and John sat listening to the car radio, straining to pick up the last few holes of the Lytham Open of 1979. 'The reception', she remembers, 'was quite appalling – but it somehow meant a lot to be able to share in the excitement surrounding Seve's win.'

On returning home, Jill took gentle aim on getting back in the county team, as much with a view to renewing old friendships as anything else. Then, when she won the Surrey championship of 1981, Diane Bailey, the county captain, recommended she should go and play in the English championship.

Jill shrugged off the suggestion but, on winning the Surrey championship again the following year, she dutifully headed for the English at Brancepeth Castle and there reached the quarter-finals. She lost to Pat Hunt, a policewoman who, being well trained in the matter of how to act in a crisis, chipped in at the twenty-second.

On the strength of her last-eight finish, Jill was given a place in the Home Internationals of that year at Burnham and Berrow. It was a week when her competitive fibre was tested to the full as she came down the stretch with the England–Scotland match depending on the result of her singles with Pam Wright, who would go on to become a Rookie of the Year on America's LPGA tour.

With the pink jerseys of her watching team-mates swimming before her eyes, Jill survived a nearly-holed chip from the Scot at the seventeenth before winning on the home green. She was warmly congratulated on the way she had lifted her game to meet the circumstances, but few appreciated that the best was yet to come. . . .

At Silloth, the following year, Jill won the British championship, 'an event which I had always seen, and still see, as something other people win.' This, in turn, led to her trio of appearances in the Curtis Cup wherein she won a highly commendable eight points in twelve starts.

As she examined her golf before and after Jedda, so Jill realised why she was a more effective player on her return. 'Before Jedda,' she admits, 'I would get het-up or depressed about my game. Seldom did I hit on a happy medium. In other words, I was thoroughly boring about it all. After I had been away, I realised that golf wasn't everything. In such circumstances, I thrived on the support I would get from John and the children'.

Also, she was in the right frame of mind to ponder, to her advantage, on what John Jacobs had said about the practice a player does today, 'being neither for today, nor for tomorrow, but for next year and the year after.'

It was after the 1988 Curtis Cup that Jill decided that her second innings, as a tournament player, was at an end. She would play no more in the major championships, although she was happy enough to battle on at county level. Indeed, she won her eleventh county title in 1989 and her twelfth in 1991.

No one was surprised when, in 1990, she was chosen to follow

Diane Bailey as captain of the Great Britain and Ireland team for the Curtis Cup at Somerset Hills, New Jersey. They lost 14–4 but, as was to be expected, Jill wasted no time in identifying the very real problems the players had had on the swift greens and in taking practical action on her return home.

In 1991, during her year as Chairman of the English Ladies Golf Association, she made a point of ensuring that all ELGA events were played on slicker putting surfaces in order that the next generation of Curtis Cup players would not be similarly thrown.

As Jill was on the point of demitting the chairman's office at the end of 1991 and, at the same time, moving further away from her playing days and up the administrative ladder by becoming an LGU deputy, so there was a delightful, if disorientating, moment for her at Surrey's AGM.

Molly Gourlay, before she died, had asked that one of her trophies be put to good use in the county which had been so much the centre of her golfing life. Surrey officialdom, by way of a response, had instigated the Molly Gourlay Award for the county's player of the year. As the time drew near for it to be handed over, so Jill allowed her thoughts to drift to the list of up-and-coming candidates who might possibly qualify for this particular honour. All of a sudden, the 1991 Surrey champion was woken from her reverie. The winner's name was one she had not even considered . . . her own.

ANGELA UZIELLI

Angela Uzielli, as I wrote on the morning she reached the final of the 1990 English Women's championship at Rye, is an out-and-out amateur fuelled by a love for the game and its gossip.

In her own way, during that week in Sussex she did as much for the cause of over fifties as a Joan Collins, having the better of one young player after another *en route* to making off with the trophy. Her husband, who in 1965 had won the President's Putter at Rye, was in the gallery, as were her two children, Michael and Caroline.

Where Angela scored was in the matter of shot-making. The three-quarter irons she was hitting across the burnished turf were her speciality: serviceable rather than spectacular shots which time after time left her within one-putt range of the hole. Then, when it came to the putting, she was lethal with an old blade putter given to her by Colonel Tony Duncan, a former Welsh International and Walker Cup player who had followed her progress since junior county days.

On the strength of her success at Rye, Angela was given a place in England's team for the 1990 Home Internationals at Hunstanton, the course where, as a child, she had learned the art of links golf.

The oldest member of that side by a little matter of twenty-seven years, it was interesting to see how she operated *vis-à-vis* the younger generation. Where, for example, her team-mates set much store by their yardage charts, Angela explained that she had little or no faith in such figures, always preferring, 'to see the shot and to smell it'.

From Hunstanton, there was something of a *volte-face* as she headed for a British Women's Senior championship at Harrogate where she was the youngest player afield. Having defeated Helen Dobson in the English championship semi-final and Linzi Fletcher in the final, she won the Seniors by three shots from Lincolnshire's Anne Thompson. And what added to the poignancy of it all was that her mother, Peggy Carrick, was the concurrent winner of the Over 70 award.

Angela's own theory as to why, at fifty, she should have had so great a golfing year had its origins, somewhat improbably, in the family swimming pool. It was while she had been cleaning the water – in the summer of 1988 – that the pressure gauge had blown its top, the gadget cannoning into her left thumb and breaking it. When, a little ahead of time, she returned to the golf course, she donned a glove to cushion the pain. Besides doing that very effectively, it helped her to hang on to the club rather better in wet weather and when it was hot.

Angela, who repeated her Senior's win in 1991 at Ladybank, in the same week that her daughter, Caroline, was teeing off on her first year at the nearby St Andrews University, will tell you that she is longer now than she was in her twenties. In those days, she would find herself consistently out-hit – often by as much as twenty to thirty yards – by players such as Mary Everard and Julia Greenhalgh.

Knowing there had to be an explanation, she sought out Keith Macdonald, the professional at the Berkshire. He confirmed that she had it in her to be as long as the next player. It was her grip, he said, which was causing the problem. Her right hand was too much on top of the club and her hands were simply not working together.

After mastering Macdonald's recommendations, she found herself up with almost everyone except Laura Davies. Today, this winner of a dozen Berkshire titles still has length to spare off the tee, but reckons that she is a club shorter than the so-called professional amateurs with her irons.

Many, including such a demon holer-out as Michael Bonallack, have found that putting becomes increasingly difficult over the years. Angela, for her part, has not suffered on this score, even if she acknowledges that she does not have quite the same relish for the four and five footers as she had, say, when she won the British Women's championship of 1977.

As she steps on to a green, she is given to intoning, 'Whatever else I do, I mustn't three putt.' It has worked remarkably well, even if that latter-day phenomenon, the sports psychologist, might not be too impressed by this example of the Power of Negative Thinking.

With the trophy having been stolen at the start of the week, Angela Uzielli received a Harrogate men's monthly medal goblet for winning the 1990 British Senior Championship

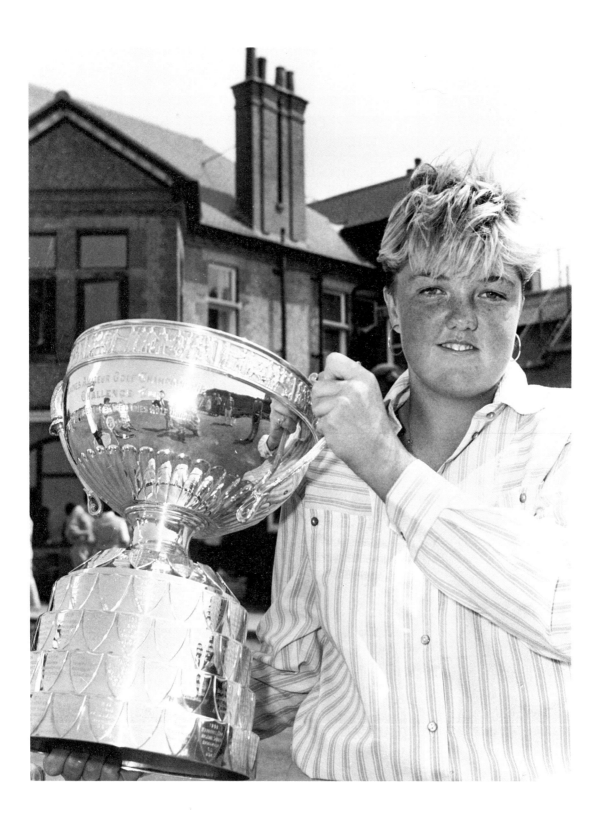

Helen Dobson, who in 1989 dominated the amateur game in a manner which put everyone in mind of Joyce Wethered's supremacy in the 1920s

CHAPTER NINETEEN

Helen Dobson

Helen Dobson owns to having had something of a premonition before the 1989 season in which she won the English Women's championship, the British, the English Girls' and the British Stroke-Play. In that order.

It came on the eve of the English at Burnham and Berrow when she was out with friends.

'You'll win this,' said one among them, lightly.

Never one to boast, the then eighteen-year-old Helen greeted the suggestion with a disbelieving smile and a couple of self-deprecating cracks. What she was saying to herself, on the other hand, was altogether different. 'Yes,' came her silent proclamation, 'I shall win.'

Those winning vibes were reinforced with each of her practice rounds. Then, in the qualifying stages, came further indications of what was to come when she handed in scores of 69 and 72 against the par of 75.

Though she had never previously won anything outwith the girls' arena, Helen topped the qualifiers by a yawning nine-shot margin. Her golf in the match-play stages continued in the same enchanted vein as she won the title without ever going farther than the fifteenth.

Runner-up to Sarah Sutton in the ensuing Astor Salver at the Berkshire, Helen won the Wentworth Scratch Cup on the following day, the result being decided on a count-back involving Jill Thornhill. 'It was a bit hard on Jill,' recalled Helen, whose memory of the situation was that she would never have featured but for a putting tip offered by Jill during their practice round.

On to the British at Hoylake where Helen gave every indication that her good run had gone up in smoke when, on the first of the two qualifying days, she hit two balls out of bounds off the first tee. She was out of bounds again later in the round but, to her eternal credit, posted nothing worse than an 81. Her second round 77, in which she played the first hole in precisely the same way she had done the day before, enabled her to qualify for the match-play with just a shot to spare. 'As English champion,' said Helen, in endeavouring to explain her somewhat shaky start, 'I arrived at Hoylake with the rather negative thought that it would be bad for me not to qualify.'

Relieved though she was, the Lincolnshire golfer was unable to relax for a second in her first-round match with Mary McKenna. . . . Three up with five to play, she eventually had to hole from twenty-five feet to shake off Ireland's top golfer at the eighteenth. 'After what had happened to me at the first in the qualifying stages, I was simply dreading going down the nineteenth,' she confessed, wincing still at the thought.

Whereas, at Burnham and Berrow, she felt that her performance had tailed off in the final which she won to the tune of 4 and 3 against the useful Simone Morgan, Helen found herself improving with each passing day in the British. She won a great match with Catriona Lambert in the semi-finals and was then five under par after nine holes on her way to defeating Elaine Farquharson by 6 and 5 in the final. 'I have never,' she says, 'hit the ball better than I did that day. Everything was right.'

Helen, a good all-round games player who is capable of playing a winning game of tennis with either hand, swapping the racket around according to how she sees the shot, notched her next success in the Bridget Jackson Bowl at Handsworth. And the next in the English Girls' at Edgbaston. There were those who said she should have been playing in the concurrent British Open, rather than among the juniors, because she would learn far more from competing alongside the professionals.

An out-and-out competitor, save where her schoolwork had been concerned, Helen did not want to take what she thought would be the easy option. She knew that the more difficult test was to win among her contemporaries, 'all of whom were after me'. Moreover, since she was eighteen, this was her last chance to play in the English Girls' championship.

Qualifying with rounds of 71 and 73, Helen missed the eight footer she needed to be out in 29 in her first round against the promising Nicola Buxton. Hardly unexpectedly, that was the match in which her golf was at its zenith; her memories of the final, by contrast, were of an uncomfortably close clash with Alison MacDonald.

Contrary to everyone's predictions, the English Stroke-Play championship at Hollinwell was not won by Helen Dobson. But it was Helen's health, rather than her golf, which let her down. Having returned a flushed and feverish 77 in the first round, Helen sought out a doctor who exclaimed, at once, that here was as severe a case of tonsilitis as he had ever seen. Helen was not so sick as to desist from pointing out that she had no tonsils.

The medication which she requested and which she was prescribed were rather different. . . . What she had in mind was a pot of pills which would effect an overnight cure and enable her to tee up the next day and make up for that first round 77. The doctor, on the other hand, refused to recommend anything other than a fortnight's rest. An exasperated Helen drove home where, as you would imagine, she was not too sorry to be able to curl up in her bed.

She did not play in the Intermediate championship but came back to win the British Women's Stroke-Play championship at Southerness. As she herself is the first to say, her swing that week was in need of a service, but the way in which she came from behind to defeat the Australian Nadine Hall in the final round was nothing short of spectacular. Two to the rear of the visitor after nine holes, she had five birdies between the eleventh and the sixteenth to win by two strokes.

Still to come were the *Daily Mail* Foursomes, which she won in partnership with Moira Wilson, and the World Fourball championship in Brazil in which she played alongside Elaine Farquharson, the Scottish champion of that year.

After that, it was a matter of picking up one award after another. The Midlands gave her a memento, as did Lincolnshire and the LGU, whose presentation consisted of a silver club and pearl ball brooch, an exquisitely evocative little item in which Helen will delight all her days. On the same tack, she was made Avia Golfer of the Year at a ceremony at which Lord Deedes, in making the award, picked out her performance in winning the *Daily Mail* Foursomes. The gist of his message was that it told much about Helen's character that she should have found time, amongst golf's majors, to meet the demands of this lighter event.

Much though she enjoyed the award circuit, Helen had still to be convinced that she had done anything out of the ordinary: 'I thought that I would be able to go out and do the same again in 1990. . . .'

She still thought as much as she set out to defend her English title at Rye – even though she was troubled by the tennis elbow which was to ruin her entire year. Ultimately, she lost in the semi-finals to Angela Uzielli. Then, and only then, did she look back on her 1989 season and say a heartfelt 'Wow!'.

11th European Ladies Team Championship, Dublin, 1979. From left to right: Miss Susan Gorman, Miss Claire Nesbitt, Miss Rhona Hegarty, Mrs Maire O'Donnell (captain), Miss Mary McKenna, Miss Maureen Madill, Miss Mary Gorry

The winning Great Britain team at the 1991 Commonwealth Tournament at the Northumberland Golf Club., From left to right: Vicki Thomas, Elaine Farquharson, Catriona Lambert, Linzi Fletcher and Julie Hall

Listings

LADIES GOLF UNION

The following is a list of those officials without whose services the LGU would never have reached its first century.

PRESIDENTS

1908–21	HRH Princess Victoria of Schleswig-Holstein
1922–30	HRH Princess Helena Victoria
1931	Viscountess Rhondda
1932–38	Lady Denman
1939–60	Viscountess Astor CH
1961–63	Miss Doris Chambers OBE
1964–66	Miss D. Ferguson
1967–69	Mrs I. G. Nicholls
1970–72	Mrs H. G. Burton
1973–75	Miss M. Holdsworth MBE
1976–78	Miss M. Smyth
1979–81	Miss L. B. Clark
1982–84	Mrs M. Garrett
1985–86	Mrs J. Young
1987–88	Miss K. W. McNeil
1989–91	Mrs E. M. Bruen
1992–	Mrs C. Comboy

VICE-PRESIDENTS

Mr W. Laidlaw Purves
Mr Talbot Fair
Mr H. S. C. Everard
Mr T. Gilroy
Col. J. MacCalmont MP
Mr Horace Hutchison
Mr T. H. Miller
Mr Hall Blyth
Mr Ryder Richardson
Mr Robert Whyte
Lord Churston
Mr H. C. Kelly
Lady Alice Stanley
Mr J. L. Low
Mr Fred Hoey
Mr Bernard Darwin
Rt. Hon. Ellis Griffith PG KG MP
Mrs T. H. Miller
Hon. Rupert E. Beckett
Captain Allan MacBeth
Captain Aylmer Somerville
Sir Harold J. Reckitt Bart
Mrs F. Rogers
Mrs Franklin Thomas
Mrs J. Walter Harland
Mrs Lewis Smith
Mr Norman Boase CBE JP

Mr John Duncan
Mrs Dunlop Hill
Mrs R. J. McNair
Mr T. A. Torrance
Miss M. M. MacFarlane
Mrs D. I. Abraham JP
Mrs Townsend
Miss N. R. Lloyd-Williams
Miss Doris Chambers
Lady Fell MBE JP
Lady Heathcoat-Amory
Sir Aynsley V. Bridgland CBE
Mrs J. E. Holloway
Sir Stuart Goodwin
Nancy, Viscountess Astor CH
Miss D. Ferguson
Mrs F. H. Dickson
Mrs M. Price
Miss E. Wilson
Mrs M. Holden
Miss L. B. Clark
Miss L. H. Peters MBE
Mrs J. H. Burnett
Mrs M. Garrett
Miss K. W. McNeil
Mrs M. Young

CHAIRMEN

1930–31	Miss Huleatt	1968–69	Miss L. B. Clark
1932	Mrs P. Hodson	1969–71	Mrs J. H. Burnett
1933	Miss N. R. Lloyd-Williams	1971–72	Mrs J. S. V. Hicks OBE
1934	Mrs R. J. McNair	1972–74	Mrs R. C. Davies
1935	Miss D. I. Clark JP	1974–76	Miss G. C. Hickson
1936	Mrs P. Hodson	1976–78	Mrs F. G. M. Baker
1937–40	Miss D. I. Clark JP	1978–80	Mrs J. Young
1940–47	Mrs D. I. Abraham JP	1980–82	Mrs E. M. Winders
1947–48	Miss N. R. Lloyd-Williams	1982–83	Mrs B. B. Brewer
1948–49	Mrs R. H. Wallace Williamson	1983–84	Mrs M. P. Bauer
1949–50	Mrs Duncan	1984–85	Mrs P. B. Taylor
1950–51	Mrs Barnes	1985–86	Mrs H. Dykes
1951–53	Miss M. Holdsworth MBE	1086–87	Mrs J. V. Todd
1953–55	Lady Katherine Cairns	1987–88	Mrs J. W. Cameron
1955–57	Mrs John Beck	1988–89	Mrs R. A. C. Cobley
1957–60	Miss M. Gourlay OBE	1989–90	Miss J. B. Lawrence
1960–63	Miss M. Holdsworth MBE	1990–91	Mrs J. Neville JP
1963–65	Miss E. Shutt	1991–92	Mrs M. Anderson
1965–67	Mrs F. H. Dickson		
1967–68	Mrs T. L. Dinwiddy		

TREASURERS

1893	Miss Blanche Martin	1948–60	Mrs J. E. Holloway
1894–1908	Mrs J. H. Hulton	1960–63	Mrs M. MacDonald
1908–12	Mrs F. T. Wright	1964–73	Mrs M. Holden
1912–30	Mrs T. H. Bird	1973–80	Mrs M. Knights
1930–35	Miss Doris Chambers	1980–87	Miss C. Denneny
1935–48	Miss M. Swanston	1987–	Mrs B. M. Frazer FCA

SECRETARIES

1893–1911	Miss Isette Pearson	1857–59	Miss S. M. Bryan Smith
1912–20	Mrs Miller	1960–62	Miss M. Thornton
1920–48	Miss MacFarlane	1962–76	Miss K. Hannay
1948–54	Miss Barbara H. Hale	1976–86	Mrs G. Anderson
1954–56	Miss S. M. Bryan Smith		
	Miss G. C. Hickson (Joint Secretaries)		

ADMINISTRATORS

1984–89	Mrs A. White	1989–	Mrs A. Robertson

TOURNAMENT SECRETARIES

1976–83	Mrs Jennie Cobb	1977–	Miss Sally Hepburn

BRITISH AMATEUR CHAMPIONS 1893–1991

YEAR	VENUE	WINNER	HOME CLUB	RUNNER-UP	BY
1893	Lytham and St Anne's	Lady Margaret Scott	Costwold	Miss I Pearson	7 and 6
1894	Littlestone	Lady Margaret Scott	Costwold	Miss I. Pearson	3 and 2
1895	Portrush	Lady Margaret Scott	Costwold	Miss E. Lythgoe	6 and 5
1896	Hoylake	Miss A. Pascoe	Wimbledon	Miss L. Thompson	3 and 2
1897	Gullane	Miss E. C. Orr	North Berwick	Miss A. Orr	4 and 3
1898	Great Yarmouth	Miss L. Thomson	Wimbledon	Miss E. C. Neville	6 and 5
1899	Co Down	Miss M. Hezlet	Royal Portrush	Miss J. Magill	2 and 1
1900	Westward Ho!	Miss R. Adair	Royal Portrush	Miss E. C. Neville	6 and 5
1901	Aberdovey	Miss N. Graham	Hoylake	Miss R. Adair	3 and 2
1902	Deal	Miss M. Hezlet	Royal Portrush	Miss E. C. Neville	20th Hole
1903	Portrush	Miss R. Adair	Royal Portrush	Miss F. Walker-Leigh	4 and 3
1904	Troon	Miss L. Dod	Moreton	Miss M. Hezlet	1 hole
1905	Cromer	Miss B. Thompson	Beverley and East Riding	Miss M. E. Stuart	3 and 2
1906	Burnham	Mrs A. M. Kennion	Brighton and Hove	Miss B. Thompson	4 and 3
1907	Co Down	Miss Hezlet	Royal Portrush	Miss F. Hezlet	2 and 1
1908	St Andrews	Miss M. Titterton	Musselburgh	Miss D. Campbell	9th hole
1909	Birkdale	Miss D. I. Campbell	Musselburgh	Miss F. Hezlet	4 and 3
1910	Westward Ho!	Miss E. Grant Suttie	Sunningdale	Miss L. Moore	6 and 4
1911	Royal Portrush	Miss D. I. Campbell	Hamilton, Canada	Miss V. Hezlet	3 and 2
1912	Turnberry	Miss G. Ravenscroft	Bromborough	Miss S. Temple	3 and 2
(Final played over 36 holes after 1912)					
1913	Lytham and St Anne's	Miss M. Dodd	Moreton	Miss E. Chubb	8 and 6
1914	Hunstanton	Miss C. Leitch	Walton Hall	Miss G. Ravenscroft	2 and 1
1915–18	No Championships – Abandoned owing to Great War				
1919	Burnham and Berrow – Abandoned owing to Railway Strike				
1920	Royal Co Down	Miss C. Leith	Carlisle and Silloth	Miss M. Griffiths	7 and 6
1921	Turnberry	Miss C. Leith	Silloth	Miss J. Wethered	4 and 3
1922	Prince's, Sandwich	Miss J. Wethered	Worplesdon	Miss C. Leitch	9 and 7
1923	Burnham and Berrow	Miss D. E. Chambers	Wittal	Mrs A. Macbeth	1 hole
1924	Royal Portrush	Miss J. Wethered	Worplesdon	Mrs F. Cautley	7 and 6
1925	Troon	Miss J. Wethered	Worplesdon	Miss C. Leitch	37th hole
1926	Royal St David's	Miss C. Leitch	Carlisle and Silloth	Mrs P. Garon	8 and 7
1927	Royal Co Down	Mlle Simone de la Chaume	St Cloud, France	Miss D. Pearson	5 and 4
1928	Hunstanton	Mlle M. le Blan	Sart, France	Miss S. Marshall	3 and 2
1929	St Andrews	Miss J. Wethered	Worplesdon	Miss C. Collett	3 and 1
1930	Formby	Miss D. Fishwick	North Foreland	Miss G. Collett	4 and 3
1931	Portmarnock	Miss E. Wilson	Notts Ladies'	Miss W. Morgan	7 and 6
1932	Saunton	Miss E. Wilson	Notts Ladies'	Miss C. Purvis-Russell-Montgomery	7 and 6
1933	Gleneagles	Miss E. Wilson	Notts Ladies'	Miss D. Plumpton	5 and 4
1934	Royal Porthcawl	Mrs A. M. Holm	Troon	Miss P. Barton	6 and 5
1935	Royal Co Down	Miss W. Morgan	Rochester and Cobham	Miss P. Barton	3 and 2
1936	Southport and Ainsdale	Miss P. Barton	Royal Mid Surrey	Miss B. Newell	7 and 5
1937	Turnberry	Miss J. Anderson	Craigie Hill	Miss D. Park	6 and 4
1938	Burnham and Berrow	Mrs A. M. Holm	Troon	Miss E. Corlett	4 and 3
1939	Royal Portrush	Miss P. Barton	Royal Mid Surrey	Mrs T. Marks	2 and 1
1940–45	No Championships – Abandoned owing to World War II				
1946	Hunstanton	Mrs G. W. Hetherington	Wanstead	Miss P. Garvey	1 hole
1947	Gullane	Mrs M. Zaharias	Park Hill, USA	Miss J. Gordon	5 and 4
1948	Royal Lytham and St Anne's	Miss L. Suggs	Capital City, USA	Miss J. Donald	1 hole
1949	Royal St David's	Miss F. Stephens	Birkdale	Mrs V. Reddar	5 and 4
1950	Royal Co Down	Vicomtesse de Saint Sauveur	Morfontaine, France	Mrs G. Valentine	3 and 2
1951	Broadstone	Mrs P. G. MacCann	Tullamore	Miss F. Stephens	4 and 3
1952	Troon	Miss M. C. Paterson	Lenzie	Miss F. Stephens	38th hole

1953	Royal Porthcawl	Miss M. Stewart	Font Hill, Canada	Miss P. Garvey	7 and 6
1954	Ganton	Miss F. Stephens	Royal Birkdale	Miss E. Price	4 and 3
1955	Royal Portrush	Mrs G. Valentine	Craigie Hill	Miss B. Romack	7 and 6
1956	Sunningdale	Miss M. Smith	St Clair River, USA	Miss M. P. Jansson	8 and 7
1957	Gleneagles	Miss P. Garvey	Co. Louth	Mrs G. Valentine	4 and 3
1958	Hunstanton	Miss G. Valentine	Craigie Hill	Miss E. Price	1 hole
1959	Berkshire	Miss E. Price	Hankley Common	Miss B. McCorkindale	37th hole
1960	Royal St David's	Miss B. McIntire	Tequesto, USA	Miss P. Garvey	4 and 3
1961	Carnoustie	Mrs A. D. Spearman	Sudbury	Miss D. J. Robb	7 and 6
1962	Royal Birkdale	Mrs A. D. Spearman	Sudbury	Mrs M. F. Bonallack	1 hole
1963	Royal Co Down	Mlle B. Varangot	St Germain, France	Miss P. Garvey	3 and 1
1964	Prince's, Sandwich	Miss C. Sorensen	Janesville, USA	Miss B. A. B. Jackson	37th hole
1965	St Andrews	Mlle B. Varangot	St Germain, France	Mrs I. C. Robertson	4 and 3

(Final played over 18 holes owing to weather conditions and over 18 holes from then onwards)

1966	Ganton	Miss E. M. Chadwick	Bramall Park	Miss V. Saunders	3 and 2
1967	Royal St David's	Miss E. M. Chadwick	Bramall Park	Miss M. Everard	1 hole
1968	Walton Heath	Mlle B. Varangot	St Germain, France	Mme C. Rubin	20th hole
1969	Royal Portrush	Mlle C. Lacoste	Chantaco, France	Miss A. Irvin	1 hole
1970	Gullane	Miss D. Oxley	West Byfleet	Mrs I. C. Robertson	1 hole
1971	Alwoodley	Miss Michelle Walker	Faversham	Miss B. Huke	3 and 1
1972	Hunstanton	Miss Michelle Walker	Faversham	Mme C. Rubin	2 holes
1973	Carnoustie	Miss A. Irvin	Royal Lytham and St Anne's	Miss Michelle Walker	3 and 2
1974	Royal Porthcawl	Miss C. Semple	Allegheny, USA	Mrs M. F. Bonallack	2 and 1
1975	St Andrews	Mrs N. Syms	Broadmoor, USA	Miss S. Cadden	3 and 2
1976	Silloth	Miss C. R. Panton	Glenbervie	Miss A. Sheard	1 hole
1977	Hillside	Mrs W. J. Uzielli	Berkshire	Miss V. Marvin	6 and 5
1978	Notts Ladies'	Miss E. Kennedy	The Australian	Miss J. Greenhalgh	1 hole
1979	Nairn	Miss M. Madill	Portstewart	Miss J. Lock	2 and 1
1980	Woodhall Spa	Mrs A. Sander	Broadmoor, USA	Mrs L. Wollin	3 and 1
1981	Caernarvonshire	Mrs I. C. Robertson	Dunaverty	Miss W. Aitken	20th hole
1982	Walton Heath	Miss K. J. Douglas	Long Ashton	Miss G. Stewart	4 and 2
1983	Silloth	Mrs J. Thornhill	Walton Heath	Miss R. Lautens	4 and 2
1984	Royal Troon	Miss J. Rosenthal	Golden Valley, USA	Miss J. Brown	4 and 3
1985	Ganton	Miss L. Behan	Curragh	Miss C. Waite	1 hole
1986	West Sussex	Miss M. McGuire	Remuera New Zealand	Mrs L. Briers	2 and 1
1987	Royal St David's	Mrs J. Collingham	Notts Ladies'	Miss S. Shapcott	9th hole
1988	Royal Cinque Ports	Miss J. Furby	Masham	Miss J. Wade	4 and 3
1989	Royal Liverpool	Miss H. Dobson	Seacroft	Miss E. Farquharson	6 and 5
1990	Dunbar	Mrs J. Hall	Felixstowe Ferry	Miss H. Wadsworth	3 and 2
1991	Pannal	Mlle V. Michaud	Biarritz, France	Miss W. Doolan	3 and 2
1992					

THE CURTIS CUP 1932–1990

1932:

Great Britain and Ireland: 3½	United States: 2½
Wanda Morgan	Opal Hill
Enid Wilson	Virginia Van Wie
Mrs J. B. Watson	Helen Hicks
Molly Gourlay	Maureen Orcutt
Doris Park	Leona Pressler Cheney
Diana Fishwick	Dorothy Higbie, Reserve
Elsie Corlett	
Captain: Joyce Wethered	Captain: Glenna Collett Vare

1934:

Great Britain and Ireland: 2½	United States: 6½
Molly Gourlay	Virginia Van Wie
Pam Barton	Charlotte Glutting
Diana Fishwick	Maureen Orcutt
Wanda Morgan	Leona Pressler Cheney
Diana Plumpton	Opal Hill
Mrs J. B. Walker	Lucile Robinson
Mrs George Coats, Reserve	Aniela Goldthwaite
	Marion Miley, Reserve
Captain: Doris Chambers	Captain: Glenna Collet Vare

1936:

Great Britain and Ireland:4½	United States: 4½
Wanda Morgan	Patty Berg
Marjorie Garon	Maureen Orcutt
Pam Barton	Leona Pressler Cheney
Mrs J. B. Walker	Opal Hill
Jessie Anderson	Charlotte Glutting
Helen Holm	Marion Miley, Reserve
Phyllis Wade, Reserve	Aniela Goldthwaite, Reserve
Bridget Newell, Reserve	
Captain: Doris Chambers	Captain: Glenna Collett Vare

1938:

Great Britain and Ireland: 3½	United States: 5½
Helen Holm	Estelle Lawson Page
Clarrie Tiernan	Maureen Orcutt
Jessie Anderson	Glenna Collett Vare
Elsie Corlett	Patty Berg
Mrs J. B. Walker	Marion Miley
Phyllis Wade	Kathryn Hemphill
Nan Baird	Charlotte Glutting
Captain: Mrs R. H. Wallace-Williamson	Captain: Frances E. Stebbins

1940–46:
No Matches (World War II)

1948:

Great Britain and Ireland: 2½	United States: 6½
Jacqueline Gordon	Louise Suggs
Jean Donald	Grace Lenczyk
Philomena Garvey	Dorothy Kirby
Zara Bolton	Dorothy Kielty
Maureen Ruttle	Estelle Lawson Page
Val Reddan	Polly Riley
Helen Holm	
Mrs A. C. Critchley, Reserve	
Captain: Doris Chambers	Captain: Glenna Collett Vare

1950:

Great Britain and Ireland 1½	United States: 7½
Jean Donald	Dorothy Germain Porter
Jessie Valentine	Beverly Hanson
Frances Stephens	Helen Sigel
Elizabeth Price	Peggy Kirk
Philomena Garvey	Dorothy Kielty
Jeanne Bisgood	Dorothy Kirby
	Polly Riley
	Grace Lenczyk
Captain: Mrs A. C. Critchley	Captain: Glenna Collet Vare

1952:

Great Britain and Ireland: 5	United States: 4
Jean Donald	Dorothy Kirby
Elizabeth Price	Grace DeMoss
Frances Stephens	Claire Doran
Jessie Valentine	Marjorie Lindsay
Moira Paterson	Polly Riley
Philomena Garvey	Pat O'Sullivan
Jeanne Bisgood	Mae Murray
Mrs P. J. McCann, Reserve	
Captain: Lady Katherine Cairns	Captain: Aniela Goldthwaite

1954:

Great Britain and Ireland: 3	United States: 6
Frances Stephens	Mary Lena Faulk
Elizabeth Price	Polly Riley
Jessie Valentine	Claire Doran
Philomena Garvey	Pat Lesser
Mrs R. T. Peel	Dorothy Kirby
Janette Robertson	Barbara Romack
Jeanne Bisgood	Grace DeMoss Smith
Captain: Mrs John B. Beck	Captain: Mrs Harrison F. Flippin

1956:

Great Britain and Ireland: 5 — United States: 4

Great Britain and Ireland	United States
Jessie Valentine	Pat Lesser
Philomena Garvey	Margaret 'Wiffi' Smith
Frances Stephens Smith	Polly Riley
Elizabeth Price	Barbara Romack
Janette Robertson	Mary Ann Downey
Veronica Anstey	Carolyn Cudone
Angela Ward	Jane Nelson
Mrs Nigel Howard, Reserve	

Captain: Mrs Sloan Bolton — Captain: Mrs Harrison Flippin

1958

Great Britain and Ireland: 4½ — United States: 4½

Great Britain and Ireland	United States
Angela Ward Bonallack	Barbara Romack
Elizabeth Price	Polly Riley
Janette Robertson	JoAnne Gunderson
Frances Stephens Smith	Anne Quast
Bridget Jackson	Barbara McIntire
Jessie Valentine	Ann Casey Johnstone
Dorothea Sommerville, Reserve	Meriam Bailey, Reserve
	Anne Richardson, Reserve

Captain: Daisy Ferguson — Captain: Mrs Charles Dennehy

1960:

Great Britain and Ireland: 2½ — United States: 6½

Great Britain and Ireland	United States
Angela Ward Bonallack	JoAnne Gunderson
Elizabeth Price	Barbara McIntire
Belle McCorkindale	Judy Eller
Janette Robertson	Anne Quast
Ruth Porter	Joanne Goodwin
Frances Smith	Ann Casey Johnstone
Philomena Garvey	Judy Bell

Captain: Maureen R. Garrett — Captain: Mrs Mildred Prunaret

1962:

Great Britain and Ireland: 1 — United States: 8

Great Britain and Ireland	United States
Angela Ward Bonallack	Anne Quast Decker
Marley Spearman	Barbara McIntire
Ann Irvin	Clifford Ann Creed
Sheila Vaughn	JoAnne Gunderson
Mrs Alastair Frearson	Jean Ashley
Ruth Porter	Ann Casey Johnstone
Jean Roberts	Judy Bell
Sally Bonallack	Phyllis Preuss

Captain: Frances Stephens Smith — Captain: Polly Riley

1964:

Great Britain and Ireland: 7½ — United States: 10½

Great Britain and Ireland	United States
Marley Spearman	Barbara McIntire
Angela Ward Bonallack	Phyllis Preuss
Bridget Jackson	Carol Sorenson
Susan Armitage	Barbara Fay White
Sheila Vaughn	JoAnne Gunderson
Ruth Porter	Nancy Roth
Joan Lawrence	Peggy Conley
Julia Greenhalgh	

Captain: Elsie Corlett — Captain: Mrs T. W. Hawes

1966:

Great Britain and Ireland: 5 — United States: 13

Great Britain and Ireland	United States
Angela Ward Bonallack	Jean Ashley
Susan Armitage	Phyllis Preuss
Belle McCorkindale Robertson	Anne Quast Welts
Joan Hastings	Barbara McIntire
Elizabeth Chadwick	Barbara Fay White Boddie
Pamela Tredinnick	Carol Flenniken
Ita Burke	Nancy Roth Syms
Marjory Fowler	Helen Sigel Wilson

Captain: Mrs Sloan Bolton — Captain: Dorothy Germain Porter

1968:

Great Britain and Ireland: 7½ — United States: 10½

Great Britain and Ireland	United States
Belle Robertson	Shelley Hamlin
Ann Irvin	Anne Quast Welts
Margaret Pickard	Mary Lou Dill
Vivien Saunders	Peggy Conley
Ann Howard	Phyllis Preuss
Pamela Tredinnick	Jean Ashley
Bridget Jackson	Roberta Albers
Dinah Oxley	

Captain: Mrs Sloan Bolton — Captain: Evelyn Monsted

1970:

Great Britain and Ireland: 6½ — United States: 11½

Great Britain and Ireland	United States
Dinah Oxley	Shelley Hamlin
Mary McKenna	Jane Bastanchury
Belle Robertson	Phyllis Preuss
Ann Irvin	Martha Wilkinson
Mary Everard	Cynthia Hill
Julia Greenhalgh	Jane Fassinger
Margaret Pickard	Nancy Hager
	Alice Dye

Captain: Jeanne Bisgood — Captain: Carolyn Cudone

1972:

Great Britain and Ireland: 8 — United States: 10

Great Britain and Ireland	United States
Beverly Huke	Laura Baugh
Mary Everard	Martha Wilkinson Kirouac
Belle Robertson	Jane Bastanchury Booth
Diane Frearson	Barbara McIntire

1974:

Great Britain and Ireland: 5 — United States: 13

Great Britain and Ireland	United States
Jennifer Lee-Smith	Anne Quast Sander
Carol LeFeuvre	Jane Bastanchury Booth
Mary McKenna	Carol Semple
Julia Greenhalgh	Cynthia Hill

Michelle Walker	Beth Barry	Mary Everard	Mary Budke
Mary McKenna	Hollis Stacy	Maureen Walker	Bonnie Lauer
Dinah Oxley	Lancy Smith	Tegwen Perkins	Beth Barry
Kathryn Phillips			Debbie Massey
Captain: Frances Stephens Smith	Captain: Jean Ashley Crawford	Captain: Belle Robertson	Captain: Mrs Allison Choate

1976:

Great Britain and Ireland: 6½ — United States: 11½

1978:

Great Britain and Ireland: 6 — United States: 12

Dinah Oxley-Henson	Debbie Massey	Julia Greenhalgh	Beth Daniel
Suzanne Cadden	Donna Horton	Vanessa Marvin	Brenda Goldsmith
Mary McKenna	Beth Daniel	Mary Everard	Cynthia Hill
Julia Greenhalgh	Cynthia Hill	Muriel Thompson	Lancy Smith
Ann Irvin	Nancy Roth Syms	Tegwen Perkins	Pat Cornett
Tegwen Perkins	Carol Semple	Mary McKenna	Carolyn Hill
Ann Stant	Nancy Lopez	Angela Uzielli	Noreen Uihlein
Jennifer Lee Smith	Barbara Barrow	Carole Caldwell	Judy Oliver
Captain: Belle Robertson	Captain: Barbara McIntire	Captain: Carol Comboy	Captain: Helen Sigel Wilson

1980:

Great Britain and Ireland: 5 — United States: 13

1982:

Great Britain and Ireland: 3½ — United States: 14½

Mary McKenna	Lancy Smith	Belle Robertson	Juli Inkster
Claire Nesbitt	Terri Moody	Mary McKenna	Carol Semple
Tegwen Perkins Thomas	Patty Sheehan	Kitrina Douglas	Kathy Baker
Gillian Stewart	Lori Castillo	Janet Soulsby	Lancy Smith
Maureen Madill	Judy Oliver	Gillian Stewart	Amy Benz
Carole Caldwell	Carol Semple	Jane Connachan	Cathy Hanlon
Jane Connachan	Lancy Smith	Wilma Aitken	Mari McDougall
Lynda Moore	Brenda Goldsmith	Vicki Thomas	Judy Oliver
	Mary Hafeman		
Captain: Carol Comboy	Captain: Nancy Roth Syms	Captain: Marie O'Donnell	Captain: Betty Probasco

1984:

Great Britain and Ireland: 8½ — United States: 9½

1986:

Great Britain and Ireland: 13 — United States: 5

Claire Waite	Joanne Pacillo	Lillian Behan	Kandi Kessler
Beverly New	Anne Quast Sander	Jill Thornhill	Cindy Schreyer
Jill Thornhill	Lancy Smith	Patricia Johnson	Danielle Ammaccapane
Penny Grice	Jody Rosenthal	Karen Davies	Dottie Mochrie
Mary McKenna	Mary Anne Widman	Belle Robertson	Kim Gardner
Laura Davies	Heather Farr	Mary McKenna	Kathleen McCarthy
Claire Hourihane	Penny Hammel	Vicki Thomas	Kim Williams
Vicki Thomas	Dana Howe	Claire Hourihane	Leslie Shannon
Captain: Diane Bailey	Captain: Phyllis Preuss	Captain: Diane Bailey	Captain: Judy Bell

1988:

Great Britain and Ireland: 11 — United States: 7

1990:

Great Britain and Ireland: 4 — United States: 14

Linda Bayman	Tracy Kerdyk	Helen Dobson	Brandie Burton
Julie Wade	Kathleen McCarthy Scrivner	Elaine Farquharson	Vicki Goetz
Karen Davies	Cindy Scholefield	Linzi Fletcher	Karen Nobel
Susan Shapcott	Carol Semple Thompson	Julie Wade Hall	Katie Peterson
Jill Thornhill	Leslie Shannon	Kathryn Imrie	Margaret Platt
Vicki Thomas	Caroline Keggi	Catriona Lambert	Anne Quast Sander
Shirley Lawson	Pat Cornett	Vicki Thomas	Carol Semple Thompson
	Pearl Sinn	Helen Wadsworth	Robin Weiss
Captain: Diane Bailey	Captain: Judy Bell	Captain: Jill Thornhill	Captain: Leslie Shannon

Viscount Whitelaw handing over the Stroyan Trophy to Katharine Harridge, whose English Girls' team won the Junior Home Internationals at Penrith in 1990

US WOMEN'S AMATEUR CHAMPIONSHIP

Year	Winner, Runner-up
1895	Mrs C. S. Brown / Miss N. C. Sargent
1896	Beatrix Hoyt / Mrs Arthur Turnure
1897	Beatrix Hoyt / Miss N. C. Sargent
1898	Beatrix Hoyt / Maude Wetmore
1899	Ruth Underhill / Mrs Caleb F. Fox
1900	Frances C. Griscom / Margaret Curtis
1901	Genevieve Hecker / Lucy Herron
1902	Genevieve Hecker / Louisa A. Wells
1903	Bessie Anthony / Miss J. A. Carpenter
1904	Georgianna M. Bishop / Mrs E. F. Sanford
1905	Pauline Mackay / Margaret Curtis
1906	Harriot Curtis / Mary B. Adams
1907	Margaret Curtis / Harriot Curtis
1908	Katherine C. Harley / Mrs T. H. Polhemus
1909	Dorothy I. Campbell / Mrs Nonna Barlow
1910	Dorothy I. Campbell / Mrs G. M. Martin
1911	Margaret Curtis / Lillian B. Hyde
1912	Margaret Curtis / Mrs Nonna Barlow
1913	Gladys Ravenscroft / Marion Hollins
1914	Mrs Katherine Harley / Elaine V. Rosenthal
1915	Mrs Florence Vanderbeck / Mrs William A. Gavin
1916	Alexa Stirling / Mildred Caverly
1917–18	No Championship (World War I)
1919	Alexa Stirling / Mrs William A. Gavin
1920	Alexa Stirling / Mrs Dorothy Campbell Hurd
1921	Marion Hollins / Alexa Stirling
1922	Glenna Collett / Mrs William A. Gavin
1923	Edith Cummings / Alexa Stirling
1927	Miriam Burns Horn / Maureen Orcutt
1928	Glenna Collett / Virginia Van Wie
1929	Glenna Collett / Mrs Leona Pressler
1930	Glenna Collett / Virginia Van Wie
1931	Helen Hicks / Mrs Glenna Collett Vare, Jr.
1932	Virginia Van Wie / Mrs Glenna Collett Vare, Jr.
1933	Virginia Van Wie / Helen Hicks
1934	Virginia Van Wie / Dorothy Traung
1935	Mrs Glenna Collett Vare, Jr. / Patty Berg
1936	Pamela Barton / Maureen Orcutt
1937	Mrs Estelle Lawson Page, Jr. / Patty Berg
1938	Patty Berg / Mrs Estelle Lawson Page, Jr.
1939	Betty Jameson / Dorothy Kirby
1940	Betty Jameson / Jane S. Cothran
1941	Mrs Betty Hicks Newell / Helen Sigel
1942–45	No Championship (World War II)
1946	Mildred 'Babe' Zaharias / Mrs Clara Sherman
1947	Louise Suggs / Dorothy Kirby
1948	Grace S. Lenczyk / Helen Sigel
1949	Mrs Dorothy Germain / Dorothy Kielty
1950	Beverly Hanson / Mae Murray
1951	Dorothy Kirby / Claire Doran
1952	Jacqueline Pung / Shirley McFedters
1953	Mary Lena Faulk / Polly Riley
1954	Barbara Romack / Mary K. (Mickey) Wright
1955	Patricia A. Lesser / Jane Nelson
1956	Marlene Stewart / JoAnne Gunderson
1957	JoAnne Gunderson / Mrs Ann Casey Johnstone
1961	Mrs Anne Quast Decker / Phyllis Preuss
1962	JoAnne Gunderson / Anne Baker
1963	Mrs Anne Quast Welts / Peggy Conley
1964	Barbara McIntire / JoAnne Gunderson
1965	Jean Ashley / Mrs Anne Quast Welts
1966	Mrs JoAnne Gunderson Carner / Mrs Marlene Stewart Streit
1967	Mary Lou Dill / Jean Ashley
1968	Mrs JoAnne Gunderson Carner / Mrs Anne Quast Welts
1969	Catherine Lacoste / Shelley Hamlin
1970	Martha Wilkinson / Cynthia Hill
1971	Laura Baugh / Beth Barry
1972	Mary Budke / Cynthia Hill
1973	Carol Semple / Mrs Anne Quast Sander
1974	Cynthia Hill / Carol Semple
1975	Beth Daniel / Donna Horton
1976	Donna Horton / Marianne Bretton
1977	Beth Daniel / Mrs Cathy Sherk
1978	Mrs Cathy Sherk / Mrs Judith Oliver
1979	Carolyn Hill / Patty Sheehan
1980	Mrs Juli Simpson Inkster / Patti Rizzo
1981	Mrs Juli Simpson Inkster / Mrs Lindy Goggin
1982	Mrs Juli Simpson Inkster / Cathy Hanlon
1983	Joanne Pacillo / Sally Quinlan
1984	Deb Richard / Kim Williams
1985	Michiko Hattori / Cheryl Stacy
1986	Kay Cockerill / Kathleen McCarthy
1987	Kay Cockerill / Tracy Kerdyk
1988	Pearl Sinn / Karen Noble

1924	Mrs Dorothy Campbell Hurd	1958	Anne Quast	1989	Vicki Goetze
	Mary K. Browne		Barbara Romack		Brandie Burton
1925	Glenna Collett	1959	Barbara McIntire	1990	Pat Hurst
	Mrs Alexa Stirling Fraser		Joanne Goodwin		Stephanie Davis
1926	Mrs G. Henry Stetson	1960	JoAnne Gunderson	1991	Amy Fruhwirth
	Mrs Wright D. Goss, Jr.		Jean Ashley		Heidi Voorhees

LADIES BRITISH OPEN CHAMPIONSHIP

(Known as Weetabix Women's British Open since 1987)

YEAR	WINNER	CLUB/COUNTRY	VENUE	SCORE
1976	J. Lee Smith	Gosforth Park	Fulford	200
1977	V. Saunders	Tyrrells Wood	Lindrick	308
1978	J. Melville	Furness	Foxhills	310
1979	A. Sheard	South Africa	Southport and Ainsdale	301
1980	D. Massey	USA	Wentworth (East)	294
1981	D. Massey	USA	Northumberland	295
1982	M. Figueras-Dotti	Spain	R Birkdale	296
1983	*Not played*			
1984	A. Okamoto	Japan	Woburn	289
1985	B. King	USA	Moor Park	300
1986	I. Davies	GB	R Birkdale	283
1987	A. Nicholas	GB	St Mellion	296
1988	C. Dibnah	Australia } tie	Lindrick	290
	S. Little	South Africa }		
(Dibnah won at second play-off hole)				
1989	J. Geddes	USA	Ferndown	274
1990	H. Alfredsson	Sweden	Woburn	288
1991	P. Grice-Whittaker	GB	Woburn	284

Index

Note: Page numbers in *italics* refer to the illustrations